Copyright © 2022 Tekkan
Artwork Copyright © 2022

All rights reserved.
First Printing, 2022
ISBN 978-1-7363537-8-3

To contact Tekkan please email:
buddhaboy1289@gmail.com

Table of Contents

Everyday Mind XXI . . . . Page 1

Everyday Mind XXII . . . . Page 101

Everyday Mind XXIII . . . . Page 201

**Things that Happened at
The Poetry Workshop**. . . . . Page 258

Everyday Mind XXIV. . . . . Page 301

Of . . . . .Page 318

Rest in Peace Mike Finley . . . . Page 333

Everyday Mind XXV. . . . . Page 401

Monkey Mind . . . . Page 492

How to Read My Poems

I want to be direct in my meaning — I want people to clearly understand my meaning. My wordiness is inspired by Shakespeare, and the (aimed-for) concision is in imitation of Japanese style. Using the sonnet with the tanka, I mix the sensibility of the Occident and the Orient — which I have done by living in England, Japan, and America.

I have married the sonnet to the tanka. I tell a story in the sonnet. The story builds to a conclusion in the last line. The tanka is a commentary, or a counterpoint, to the sonnet — the combined poems have two endings.

Recently I have added limericks and doggerel into my repertoire. The limericks have a rhyme scheme but the tanka do not.

I don't punctuate much in my poetry. I want the words themselves to do the work. There is logic between words, and the forms provide structure. By not using punctuation I hope to direct readers to carefully attend to each word — to appreciate the graininess of words.

Reading my poems silently and reading them aloud may be different experiences. There's not always a pause intended at the end of the line.

Hint: *sonnets are to be recited not as lines but as phrases, and a phrase often overflows the break at the end of a line. I pause and take a breath where it seems natural for me to pause. Another person may pause differently than I do.*

Each poem is a piece of a mosaic, and it is my hope that the collection of poems forms a portrait of consciousness.

My friend, *Will Ersland*, is a wonderful artist. His cranes and owl grace this book. Jocelyn Figueroa, my daughter, is also a wonderful artist. Her fish and sunburst bring charm to this book.

I am Barry MacDonald. I received the *dharma* name *Tekkan*, which means "Iron Man," a settled practitioner of great determination.

— *Tekkan*

Everyday Mind XXI

I close my eyes
and the bright sun
turns my eyelids
red.

I sure wouldn't want to live without friends
Because easy conversation is fun
We can find things to do on the weekends
So life is joyous over the long run
But I have to watch my expectations
I need to practice giving and taking
I have to show my appreciation
Can't be the one that's always receiving
It is better to have two points of view
To have a lively and friendly debate
And maybe more or less both views are true
There's a confusing world to celebrate
To keep a friend I have to be graceful
Otherwise I could end up remorseful.

Demanding
and
expecting
is the death
of friendship.

This week I've seen a wasp and dragonflies
Today is filled with the heat of the sun
Spring is always a tonic for the eyes
Opening my windows again is fun
It's part of my life to drive around town
I watch the metamorphosis of trees
I meditate with my car windows down
I see the world parading by at ease
The leaves of trees are unfolding again
Foliage is brightly multicolored
My movement outside is carefree again
The liveliness of earth is uncovered
There comes a point with the unfolding leaves
When I rejoice with the beauty of trees.

Suddenly
effervescent
foliage dazzles
the landscape
again.

The geese and swallows and turkey vultures
The crows and eagles and the chickadees
I see them fly and they make me wonder
What would life be like to be feathery
The quality of the wind and the air
Is common to them all but each of them
Takes to their wings with a suitable flair
And they manage the blusters as they come
I see the crows get blown off of their course
I watch the geese adapt in formations
Eagles are experts at focusing force
Vultures will soar on thermal vibrations
Swallows flicker and turn like acrobats
Chickadees are delicate acrobats.

The birds are not
separate from the
air and wind and
earth and trees
and the seasons.

I believe my cellphone is wearing out
Because I have to charge it all day long
Perhaps the battery is burning out
With a replacement I could carry on
But there are faster phones on the market
With speedier internet connections
With better attractive apps to pocket
Prompting a festival of selections
Perhaps I have forgotten my passwords
Resetting them again is a hassle
Reducing me to a frustrated nerd
Lost in a technological dazzle
I like to be hypnotized by my phone
It is much more fabulous than the moon.

I would feel
practically naked
adrift and isolated
without a functioning
cellphone.

Fingers and toes — elbows knees and ankles
I flex them each day of my existence
They do so much more than merely dangle
They offer me primary assistance
I couldn't ride a bike without my knees
Couldn't have breakfast without my elbows
With ankles I can gambol at my ease
With ankles and knees I can really flow
My fingers are most handy instruments
Futzing with a cellphone and computer
For scratching they are such good implements
I can unfasten buttons as a lover
But I'm not sure what my toes are doing
Trimming toenails is excruciating.

My fingers assist
in the trimming of
toenails but I
really have to
scrunch myself.

Dandelions are appearing again
Simultaneous with creeping charlie
Asserting themselves following the rain
Dandelions are certainly hardy
I am the only one who mows my lawn
It's my weekly responsibility
For more than twenty years I've carried on
Watching dandelion fertility
I used to think of them as nasty weeds
Their presence disturbed my tranquility
I resented the puffs that spread their seeds
But I have gained some flexibility
I don't think about what I'm stepping on
Just doing what I do — mowing the lawn.

After the puffs of seeds
dissipate in spring
the persistent yellow
flowers are cheerful.

I'm learning what to do with solitude
How do I manage thinking by myself?
All my hours are filled with my attitude
How may a person be good to oneself?
For a year I've taken to watching trees
And they don't show an inch of symmetry
These are the days of the unfolding leaves
A time of natural festivity
I especially like crabapple trees
I enjoy the color of their flowers
They bloom and leaf simultaneously
I absorb their beauty and can't be sour
Feeling optimism is a power
I turn to trees almost every hour.

Even when motionless in
the absence of a wind
the trees are weirdly
expressive.

Society is divided today
With political animosity
Even during the lovely days of May
The media conveys hostility
The pandemic virus has been awful
We have shut the schools and closed businesses
A year of sickness has been terrible
Many have died but most are witnesses
We are so suspicious of each other
That our leaders are the targets of scorn
In isolation everyone suffers
So many are too furious to mourn
And yet between my friends and family
I have the grace of a community.

Some of the leaves
are almost fully
grown while others
are only budding.

I am looking forward to normalcy
When we can go to places without masks
When we can mingle again carelessly
And then I will dump my masks in the trash
Our aimed-for goal is herd immunity
Everyone needs to be vaccinated
Shots are dispersed in each community
Soon we hope to be emancipated
The New York Times has other opinions
A writer doubts our herd immunity
Too many are making bad decisions
So we will mask up indefinitely
Too many are refusing to get shots
My stomach is tied in terrible knots.

There is suspicion
that elite leadership
doesn't want to relinquish
the power of
domination.

I practice arranging thoughts into lines
Putzing in the selection of the words
Adding the ornamentation of rhymes
While admitting that the rhyming is absurd
The lines are composed of symbols and signs
Pretending to mirror reality
As if words and reality align
And the facts and my emotions agree
The left margin is making a sideline
Always anchored with capital letters
But my exuberance isn't confined
It's getting easy to burst the fetters
Every day my intentions are the same
This poetry is a light-hearted game.

The pages are composed
of numbered Houdini tricks
with words signifying
hours of frivolity.

There is a person whom I resented
Over a question of who's dominant
Our opinions are starkly divided
And on occasion I am obstinate
We have argued at social gatherings
And afterward I considered who won
When alone I found myself arguing
The consequences of fighting weren't done
Eventually I chose to walk away
Leaving behind some people whom I like
Which has led to more solitary days
But it's better than getting into fights
And now I haven't seen him for a while
Until yesterday when he waved and smiled.

I drove ahead
with much
lingering
bitterness
dissipated.

My eyesight has always been terrible
I depend totally on my glasses
In choosing frames I am fashionable
Believing that my round frames are classics
But my lenses are chipped and breaking down
A bifocal part has become fuzzy
I went to the optometrist in town
Resigned to spend a lot of my money
And he told me about my cataracts
That it's almost time to have them removed
Afterward I won't need glasses perhaps
That my vision would be so much improved
But I'm waiting to get on Medicare
Making the expense easier to bear.

I'm used to seeing
through the smudges
And nicks of my
lenses.

I make a big deal of the blooms of spring
In poetry exaggerating in
A way that I don't do in casual
Conversation with my friends because when

Something is put on the pristine whiteness
Of a page of paper or is read to
Group of people it is an occasion
For the distillation of and for the

Celebration of the periodic
Appearance of beauty punctuating
And turning the humdrum business of life
Into something special even though I

Know that between my garage and house
Only one red tulip will be blooming.

Tulips abound
about town but
I love my single
bloom by the
garage.

I am a believer in the troughs and
Crests of life having experienced the
Intimacy and the solicitude
Of love for a time which I assumed would

Continue indefinitely and now
I know how it feels to have love withdrawn
Suddenly and seemingly without a
Reason and there's anger and hurt and a

Compulsion to figure out what happened
But really there's nothing to do but to
Receive the disorientation of
A loss which is a trough on the way to

Becoming a crest while accepting the
Traumatic quality of emotion.

Each personality
leaves ripples
merging into
incessant
undulation.

It's funny how over time a person
Gets used to the way that things appear and
I have been wearing my round glasses with
Treated lenses that turn brown in sunlight

For eight or nine years and didn't notice
When they became smudged and chipped as I am
Attending to the panorama and
Metamorphosis of the earth but now

The state of my lenses and my waiting
For Medicare eligibility
Has forced me to return to an older
Pair of glasses that are almost as good

Though not as stylish and I have to raise
My chin repeatedly to see clearly.

My neck is sore and
adjusting to new motion
as I look through the
lower half of the
bifocals.

Is it hard to imagine how life must
Have appeared to Karen Carpenter who
Was a celebrated American
Singer but who could not overcome the

Self-critical and the despairing thoughts
Coming from absorbing her image in
A mirror reflecting a consciousness
Of never being good enough leading

To a compulsion to starve herself of
Nutrition to be ever slimmer than
She was eventually bringing on
Heart failure and death — it is hard to grasp

How hypnotizing and encompassing
A vision in a mirror can become.

It is hard to imagine
how life could be
without looking
into mirrors.

On the chilly days of spring I can ride
My bicycle again after watching
It leaning against my dining room wall
For the entirety of the winter

Reminding me of my captivity
Indoors and now over the Lift Bridge of
Downtown Stillwater I thrust myself up
The long incline of the hill to Houlton

Rising off of the bicycle seat and
Dancing upright on the pedals gauging
My pacing up the hill repeatedly
Over days and weeks making the ascent

A worthy cynosure of my twenty-
Mile circuit on glorious afternoons.

My high-tech bicycle
leaning against my
dining room wall is
an eloquent vision
of arrested speed.

There are spring snow crabapple trees blooming
Around Stillwater coincident with
The unfolding of leaves and already
Some of the blossoms are scattering from

The trees in the wind spreading on the streets
And the grass looking not so much like snow
To me but like confetti left over
From a parade that has passed by and the

Pristine whiteness and the delicate and
Velvety texture of petals fallen
On the ground conveys to me a tinge of
Transience and sadness as an event

That I've looked forward to for many months
Is reaching fulfillment and is going.

My years of living
in Japan habituated
me to the celebration
and the transience
of flowering trees.

Tightly wound and pink buds are appearing
On my apple trees by the driveway and
Across the yard the lilac blossoms are
Emerging as the creeping charlie and

The dandelions are already well
Established and leaves of the towering
Cottonwood are half-grown and sparkling in
The sun and I wonder at the buds of

The apple tree that are pink and yet in
Their full expression they become white and
Every year I watch the blooming of my
Yard looking for something special to say

About these predictable events and
I guess what matters is they bring me joy.

The spring leaves
are luminous with
the sun for a while
and then they lose
their luster.

Space between the trees reverberates with
The various and persistent sounds of
The birds in the morning and the extent
Of the cloudless sky is only partly

Hinted at by the towering height of
The cottonwood at the corner of my
Yard and all the emerging leaves up and
Down the cottonwood are moving in a

Chilly breeze and flickering with the light
Of the sun giving the space between the
Tree and me through which the breeze is blowing
A sensuous and an almost liquid

Quality and words cannot do justice
But can only hint at undulation.

The space about my car
left a paper-thin layer
of ice on my windshield
that I am scraping off.

So many people I know do speak of
The love of God who sustains them in a
Gentle embrace empowering them to
Overcome difficulties and answering

For them a need of reassurance and
Of strength allaying the underlying
And the nagging of doubts that cause so much
Trouble and doubts add such poignancy to

Everyday events and I'm not so much
Different only I don't pigeonhole
God inside of a personality
Directing events but I wonder how

Everything arises from emptiness
And returns so oddly to emptiness.

I believe
degrees of suffering
are various but
consciousness is
indestructible.

The space between the things of the world that
We move and live within and from which we
Witness again the awakening and
The flourishing of spring wherein the grass

Grows and the tulips and cherry trees and
And hepatica bloom and the pussy
Willows open and the robins and killdeer and
Blue herons and redwing blackbirds and the

Grackles arrive from migration and the
Mourning cloak butterflies activate from
Hibernation this space between which the
Earth is resurrected again in spring

Is space/mind arising with sensations
Fostering experience and knowledge.

The emptiness from which
space/mind emerges is
the absence of sensation
experience and knowledge.

A girl named River who has multiple
Sclerosis and uses devices to
Help her move about assisted me for
An afternoon in the composition

Of business cards enabling me to
Better present myself as a poet
Within a circle of poets that she
Knows about because she is a worthy

Poet and an artist herself and I
Enjoyed the time conjoining paintings of
An indigo bunting and a sunburst
With colored letters and numbers and with

Rounded corners and textured paper and
I will cherish the day that we made cards.

River prepared
golden milk with
assorted spices which
we had with apples
coated with peanut butter.

The time it takes for me to choose a word
That embodies a meaning worthy of
Utterance is a kind of space — like the
Distance it takes to walk from here to there —

This kind of space has a quality that
Is measured by the things that happen and
Are remembered to have happened within
The passage of time — as can be seen when

Nothing happens and then time disappears —
But when it happens that the words come with
Ease and focused fascination then there
Is an intensity and very much

Happens in a short amount of time and
Then time may lose its semblance of order.

So perhaps time/space
is relative to what
is happening in the
moment.

Some of the leaves are almost fully grown
Other trees are only starting to bud
But is anything growing on its own?
Doesn't everything depend on a tug?
My apple trees are leafing and blooming
Without a reference to a calendar
Do they grow as they do without choosing?
Do they take their cues from the atmosphere?
I let my apple trees influence me
I planted them and have watched them growing
Through the years they are pacifying me
Apple blossom scent will soon be flowing
Apple trees and lilacs bloom together
But I don't believe that they are tethered.

It's a happy
coincidence my
lilacs on the corner
bloom with my
apple trees.

A part of me enjoys a gloomy day
When the clouds are heavy and threaten rain
When high expectations are thrust astray
Because a part of me likes to complain
I may be bad-tempered and that's OK
I am stuck at the moment and feeling strain
I can give myself a little leeway
Because elation is hard to maintain
It's good that my plans are in disarray
What is best for me I don't ascertain
I am happy to toss mistakes away
I'm just being moody — I'm not insane
I may turn my thinking without delay
Being jubilant again is child's play.

I can let the drama
drain out of my head
like air escaping
a balloon.

I waste a lot of time composing rhymes
Do you think I'm making the world better?
Poetry isn't a dreadful pastime
Cleaner than fixing a carburetor
And I try to finish before lunchtime
Afterward I work on my newsletter
No one can become a poet full time
Not without ending up as a debtor
Christopher Marlow is my paradigm
Another Elizabethan writer
But I cover the news in the meantime
I'm always looking for new subscribers
The daily news just encapsulates crime
I want a diversion from all that grime.

We have to do something
With our time —
half rhyme
eye rhyme
ragtime
pantomime.

You surely are a beautiful woman
With a delicate neck and slender shoulders
Which comport so well with ample bosoms
A striking effect on this beholder
You're posing with a careless nonchalance
Projecting unconscious self-confidence
A vision for a passion to ensconce
I savor looking without consequence
Obviously a force to contend with
A formidable conjuror of love
A risky obsession to befriend with
And once smitten so hard to dispose of
It is fetching what you do with your eyes
I don't want to believe they're telling lies.

We haven't even
spoken a word to
each other yet you've
seized my attention
with your eyes.

Do you know the word "equanimity"?
It means a person possessing balance
It is protection from fragility
Being quiet and stable is a talent
I know what it's like to be caught by love
Always desiring — living with tension
It's a trap I'm happy to be free of
It's not fun to engender suspicion
My trouble is I become possessive
Then I wonder does she really love me?
Launching thinking that becomes obsessive
I get so encumbered I can't be free
Then I start to question my dignity
My life gets tangled in perplexity.

Could I love without
engendering
possession and
suspicion?

I was given the *dharma* name "*Tekkan*"
In a ceremony involving vows
My name comes from the Zen master Dogen
His inspiration moves our Buddhist vows
He's a central figure in history
As the founder of Zen within Japan
Maybe he graces my trajectory
The name "*Tekkan*" signifies "Iron Man"
A disciple with determination
That is what my name indicates in me
I've been practicing without cessation
I do my meditation happily
But most of all I watch how I'm thinking
I aim my practice towards balanced living.

Equanimity
compassion
benevolence
altruistic joy
is the way.

Thank you — reader — for following my words
You are lending me the use of your eyes
Perhaps we are both a couple of nerds
It's a fancy game to epitomize
I would also like to borrow your heart
Maybe I could ask you to sympathize?
I turn curiosity into art
With queries and quizzes I synthesize
I'd like to explore the nature of love
Is its basic function to harmonize?
Is it also predatory? Kind of
Its primary trick is to mesmerize
To snare to burden and to tantalize
And all the while we tend to rhapsodize.

I don't want to minimize
And rather not maximize
Love is biblical
And formidable
And does tend to pulverize.

Imagine my surprise when she calls me
I was doing my work reading essays
As first she says that she's a divorcée
Which is more than a hint she wants to play
She says that her ex can be quite nasty
He expected much — she couldn't obey
Her married life was boring and messy
And she heard me speaking the other day
I seemed so intelligent and carefree
She's curious about what I have to say
She would like to get together with me
She suggested we meet and have coffee
Asking "Which are the days that I am free?"

I do distrust fantasy
I'm wary of vanity
But she is so bold
Over a threshold
Beyond rationality.

I am having trouble concentrating
The daily news has lost my interest
That phone conversation was breathtaking
And now my thinking is incoherent
I would rather not be fantasizing
I can see her tricks — I'm not ignorant
I have my essays to be editing
But I find myself a little listless
She certainly is disorienting
I could almost profess to be witless
I can see myself prevaricating
It's getting hard to focus on business
I'd like to say that this is irritating
But in my heart I know it's exciting.

She is precipitating
I am participating
Could this be love?
Coming from above?
As I am fantasizing.

She was brash to call me and I was shocked
I didn't anticipate such a move
And I was stimulated as we talked
The fact that she reached out to me is huge
She's lonely and newly separated
Desiring to know how I'm getting by
She's sad and wants to be educated
She thinks I'm cheerful and wants to know why
How is it that troubles don't get me down?
Her husband told her so many damn lies
She certain that he's been fooling around
And I'm the lucky guy who caught her eye
Suddenly my life is turned upside down
I am different but I don't know how.

I am appreciated
And now I am elated
My heart is beating
My mind is racing
I've become captivated.

This is the time of the year for lovers
The sun's bursting with energy again
So much liveliness to rediscover
And I'm feeling exuberant again
Flowering trees are at the fullest bloom
Most of the leaves are almost fully grown
Warm summer breezes are arriving soon
I may find a love that I've never known
It's so nice to be appreciated
My life has taken on a sudden turn
Which I could not have anticipated
What's coming next I really can't discern
Been a long time since I've felt so happy
I won't say more because I'll get sappy.

Now I am speculating
My heart is palpitating
And I can't sit still
As I'm feeling thrills
I am anticipating.

And now I have her number on my phone
We're meeting at Caribou for coffee
My expectations are not overblown
I intend to be a real softie
I don't remember feeling this before
A superfluity of energy
I've reached a state of opening new doors
But now my mind is wandering strangely
I'm questioning — what is she really like?
And will our conversation be easy?
I'd like to believe that we think alike
I'm getting hints that she may be teasy
She is a cutie with an easy smile
She comports herself with a sense of style.

Life is now propitious
I'm suddenly ambitious
I'm having a yen
Apart from my Zen
I'm feeling adventurous.

I am fine and I have my work to do
I have to settle and to concentrate
There are essays to edit in a queue
I need to clear my head to operate
The essays are about society
I have to correct syntax and grammar
It's important to show sobriety
Because we address serious matters
Love is very fine but now I'm busy
I just want to sit and to do my work
Can't let myself entertain a tizzy
This obsessive passion is quite a quirk
A week ago I lived differently
Considered affairs indifferently.

I like articulation
And also speculation
Want to be useful
And also truthful
I don't like agitation.

I am getting my second shot in a
Walmart about twenty miles away and
Then I'll be fully vaccinated
And immune to the pandemic virus

And free to go in most places without
Wearing a mask which has turned into a
Symbol of fear and of submission to
Bureaucratic edict which would have been

Easier to take if the mask pushers
Hadn't allowed themselves liberties that
They wouldn't allow others and so a
Threshold is passing a significant

Tension is lifting and I welcome a
Taste of anticipated normalcy.

Like dominoes
falling the stores
about town are
lifting mask
mandates.

Under the threat of impending rain I
Ride my bicycle like a greyhound in
Stride and I'm proud of myself until a
Rider comes along and passes me by

Showing me there's room for improvement and
I notice the leaves of the trees and the
Black glossy feathers of the grackles at
A high place near the bridge and next to a

Cornfield I see that the willow that serves
As a landmark is fully leaved again
And is gracefully flowing and then I
Spot a redwing blackbird fly and perch on

A slender stem of a plant that I would
Have thought was too thin to support it.

The blackbird
knows better than
I the bearing
capacity of stems.

As I am moving about I can take
A moment and gaze at the cottonwood
On my corner looking up and into
The air to see the leaves up and down the

Tree fully grown now and turning in a
Breeze which is only a slight whiff of a
Wind and I can listen to the sound of
The breeze moving the leaves and I can hear

The peaceful soothing sound of the wind in
The leaves which I haven't heard since the fall
And then I wouldn't really have noticed
Because the sighing of the leaves in the

Wind happening all summer long was a
Sound I had gotten used to and ignored.

Seeing and hearing
cottonwood leaves
wafting in a breeze
again is an interlude
in a busy day.

The second shot of the vaccine is the
One reputed to cause just a touch of
The illness and it was so with me as
I had a fever and soreness in the

Morning afterward so that I slept a
Little longer reacquainting myself
With the way the world looks from the view of
A fevered mentality resembling

A hall of funhouse mirrors reflecting
Back to me the incidents of my life
In distorted and grotesque images
Which are only mildly disturbing as

By now I know such views are only a
Trick of the mind unworthy of notice.

The world looks
very different
once I drink coffee
and get moving
again.

Rain is pounding on the roof and running
Along the gutters and the damp chilly
Air is pouring through the open windows
And rain is descending in a deluge

And the light of the morning is dimmed by
Its sudden intensity — and the view
Of pines and of the neighboring homes is
Obscured by the sheets of the falling rain —

And it's nice sheltering inside my home
Listening to the rhythmical sound of
The rain spattering on concrete seeing
The rain being absorbed into the grass

And with every inhalation of breath
My nose is filling with the smell of rain.

And just a few
moments later
the rain becomes
a gentle patter.

The media of America is
Leveraging the news and inspiring
Bitterness by demonizing people
And the schools and universities are

Aggressively ideological
Condemning historical figures and
Lawyers and judges are advocating
Political agendas apart from

The impartial application of law
And celebrity athletes and actors
Are assuming roles as political
Activists and there's a new and scary

Intolerance in America for
A genuine diversity of thought.

In American cities
violent mobs are
seizing the initiative
and taking control.

After days of rain soaking into the
Soil the grass is upthrusting and needs to
Be mowed today or it will grow enough
To clog the blades of the mower and the

Yard will be unmanageable as we
Are having hours of resplendent sun
With the drifting of scattered clouds followed
By the domination of pelting and

Spattering rain cooling the humid air
And with the returning sun birds emerge
Blue jays cardinals grackles woodpeckers
Robins and now and again I see the

Graceful flight of a single or a pair
Of sandhill cranes slicing through the moist air.

The roots of grasses
hedges and trees are
drinking water and
minerals and the leaves
are tasting sunlight.

It is a pleasantry of living that
One can arrange the letters of words on
A thin sheet of paper bound together
On the left side to form the pages of

A book in an attempt to glimpse and to
Capture the essences of life in a
Distillation of consciousness applied
To experience using syllables

And rhythm composing a language that
Hopefully performs a trick very much
Like an acrobat launched and tumbling in
The air within a millisecond poised

With flying and open hands to be grasped
And caught by a comprehending reader.

I live for moments
when the conduits of
words are left behind in
loving comprehension.

He calls me to let me know he's gotten
An accounting job and can expect a
Good salary with better benefits
And he's talkative which is a turn from

The one-word responses that he often
Gave to questions and he has friends who he
Meets with and he's prospering with his
Business degree and he wants to buy a

Condominium with a mortgage and
We share our views of the difficulties
Of politics which is a pleasure that
We understand each other and those years

When my son was troubled and beyond my
Ability to reach may be over.

Thousands of miles
away in Juneau
Alaska Joshua is
becoming
himself.

So many memories lie unsummoned
Only needing prompting to come back
To consciousness years of unhappiness
Between Yoshiko my ex-wife and I

And Joshua disharmony lasting
Almost thirty years but Joshua wants
To vacation with his mom in Japan the
Country of his birth returning her to

The home of so many complicated
Memories and what surprises me is
That Joshua on his initiative
Is intending a magnificent and

A healing gesture of reunion that
I could never have anticipated.

Joshua intends
to accompany
his mom on a
healing journey
of reunion.

I know what keeps me optimistic and
Young at heart is that I look outside of
Myself watching the intricacies of
The world and I don't have to go on a

Vacation to find reasons worthy of
Gratitude because I am calm enough
To be able to hear the sighing of
The wind in the leaves and to allow a

Swelling peacefulness come over me that
Naturally accompanies the sight
And the sound of leaves rustling in a breeze
No matter what is happening within

The human world the majesty of trees
In motion is cause for celebration.

Maybe if my thoughts are
subdued enough
I could spot a
rose-breasted grosbeak.

Hulk Hogan was a gesticulating
Good guy while Rowdy Roddy Piper was
A clever and insulting rogue and the
Undertaker was an eerie silent

Character who was benevolent and
Stone Cold Steve Austin was a working-class
Hero and Andre the Giant had a
Child-like simplicity and they were all

Operatically acrobatically
Entertaining stadiums full of fans
Bellowing body slamming and smacking
Each other with metal folding chairs and

Like the Gods of Olympus they performed
Edifying morality fables.

The World Wrestling
Entertainment show
is America's
Mount Olympus.

You keep me waiting and I am bemused
Waiting for you to get off of the phone
I am a little put off and confused
Standing awkwardly quietly alone
I'm sure you noticed that I have arrived
As I anxiously await our first date
Your sudden busyness does seem contrived
So what else am I to anticipate?
It seems you have a good sense of timing
You know how long to keep me suspended
Then you turn the mood by sweetly smiling
My budding frustration is upended
Part of me recognizes clever tricks
And part of me ignores — getting a kick.

I am excitedly
matched with a
voluptuous
temptress.

There's excitement in being overmatched
Encountering fresh and challenging games
Stimulated yes but not overwhelmed
I am not unskilled in using my brain
She's wispy slender and possesses grace
Getting divorced is difficult for her
She has such an innocent pixie face
There are lawyer expenses to incur
Her husband is now an alcoholic
How she asks do I live without boozing?
Living sober I say is a frolic
It's an unburdened life of my choosing
I am careful not to gaze at her breasts
Taking only glimpses I think is best.

She is genuinely
engaged and
interested in my
spiritual
practice.

She knows her husband isn't a nice guy
But he's been a very good provider
She's put up with his drinking and his lies
She's wanted to help but he's defied her
He is an electrical engineer
They had a large and luxurious house
Things have gotten ugly over the years
Until now he's no better than a louse
Their two grown sons have come to despise him
They are out of the house and on their own
They're exhausted and disgusted with him
The family cohesion has broken down
She's much happier living by herself
And he can drink all he wants by himself.

Her dad died early
of alcoholism and
her ex-husband's
an ugly drunk.

She knows people who have heard me speaking
She's heard I'm eloquent and effective
That I manage to live without drinking
That I'm compassionate and reflective
She wants to learn spiritual principles
And what sobriety is based upon
Her former life has made her cynical
Faith in religiosity is gone
I am in a peculiar position
A place beyond my anticipating
No longer burdened by inhibitions
Now I know my heart is palpitating
I've not been so flattered and exalted
Can't remember being so excited.

I'm supposed to be mindful
of equanimity
but such is not my
emerging
propensity.

Is this disembodied experience?
I'm becoming so infatuated
She's tantalizingly mysterious
She's passionate and yet understated
Daydreaming of her is luxurious
During the night my thoughts are excited
Losing sleep is creating weariness
I have a fear of being deflated
Perhaps she is just being curious
And her affections are calculated
Maybe I am driven by prurience
Are my possibilities limited?
Is both lusting and loving spurious?
My state of being is precarious.

Is it love or lust
that's intoxicating?
If there were medicine
would I take it?

Are such strong passions deleterious?
My serenity is dissipated
Complicating my Zen experience
But shouldn't loving be celebrated?
I'm finding my moods can be various
When doubting myself I'm devastated
Balancing feelings is precarious
Such crazy emotions are serrated
And then I find myself gregarious
Pondering her praise makes me elated
More than happy — I am delirious
I suspect I'm overstimulated
Now I am so oddly situated
But isn't love to be venerated?

In the lotus posture
a position of the
body I've practiced
more than thirty years
I must appear — serene.

To call or not to becomes a question
How to measure the weightiness of time
Her words and gestures — full of suggestions
I'm tending to business in the meantime
I am reading the daily narratives
The pressure of politics is extreme
Freighted with dishonest declaratives
The daily hypocrisy is routine
And how could I bring her to understand?
When it's taken me years to learn the game
The phony slogans are absorbed offhand
But the sound bites and truth are not the same
I do care about our society
And that may be a liability.

To the
uninitiated
making myself
understood
is difficult.

Having opinions is only human
We take possession without much thinking
I try to penetrate my delusions
To follow guidelines without much clinging
I begin each day with meditation
I watch thoughts come and let them dissipate
Part of me laughs at my own gyrations
I let my ideas proliferate
Love and politics are complicated
How could I not become a partisan?
I want results to be consummated
Propaganda may be bipartisan
Strong emotion is intoxicating
A lovely woman is hypnotizing.

A turkey vulture
warms his wings
circling in a
sunny thermal.

Infatuation comes in any season
And the brilliance of spring skies is lovely
Love has nothing to do with my reason
Watching my befuddlement is funny
I'm absorbed in love riding my bicycle
And propelled by the wind I'm riding swiftly
I am passionate — I am physical
And I am riding precipitously
Spring is awakening — with wide open skies
Now that swallows have returned to the fields
Their adroit maneuvers dazzle my eyes
They turn and dart and then suddenly wheel
I fly through the country over the ridge
Speed in the air on the Crossing Bridge.

Love is rippling
the vast river far below —
the sky is cloudless
and the river is cloudless
they are both shining blue.

Perhaps I'm being a bit of a clown
Being overly infatuated
And I'm afraid of being let down
I know what it's like to be deflated
My juices are flowing — capturing me
Something I hadn't anticipated
My obsession with her won't let me be
Nothing I'm doing is calculated
Thank God I'm not a judge or a lawyer
My rationality is compromised
I'll operate more cleverly later
Perhaps I'm being manipulated
Is she — or am I — doing this to me?
Is this a heaven? Or catastrophe?

My dear — you should see
me poised within the lotus
posture appearing
serenely composed within
such passionate vibrations.

Why would someone choose a nasty husband?
She did say that he's a good provider
She is clever and doesn't get flustered
She may be attracted to aggressors
And then why is she attracted to me?
She is intelligent and so am I
She wants to learn something from me maybe
And so I wonder what that signifies
I'm all about being poised and open
She knows that I'm seeking liberation
Some of us hit bottom and are broken
There's a saving grace in desperation
To do meditation isn't easy
This girl is coquettish and she's teasy.

A part of me knows
that I want to be needed
to be desired
by the opposite sex and
now I'm hungering again.

There's a paradox in liberation
At least of the type that I am seeking
Trying too hard creates separation
I'd like to give up the habit of grasping
There is the initial desperation
A lingering period of suffering
That's enough to inspire frustration
That culminates in a new beginning
From there what's needed is relaxation
A peace apart from unending striving
Fascination with subtle vibrations
There is patience to be cultivating
I want to surf with my motivations
I would like to balance with emanations.

Romantic love and
political victory
may be delusions
to be grasped only for a
moment before they dissolve.

A violin is tuned exquisitely
And then the music is quite eloquent
I don't put much faith in passivity
Believing right effort is relevant
I'd like to act with sensitivity
So is playing politics negligent?
It should be done with selectivity
My motives need to be benevolent
But can I keep my objectivity?
Or could I myself be malevolent?
There's confusion in relativity
Opponents are commonly arrogant
I need my strength and flexibility
I'd like to keep a sense of etiquette
But being passive is a detriment.

There could be peace in
doing my best and leaving
the results up to
cosmic vibrations beyond
anyone's permanent grasp.

The birds are noisy before the sunrise
Just listening is intoxicating
Their joyful persistence does hypnotize
But in truth the males are advertising
They are using voices to lionize
Each of the males is fiercely competing
When conniving for mates they dramatize
The allure of females must be enticing
Is my loving a lusting in disguise?
Even so is that disqualifying?
Are my motives getting crosswise?
Don't want to stop my anticipating
And I don't want to overanalyze
My newfound romance is energizing.

It's necessary
for a mommy and daddy
buddha to combine
before a baby buddha
can properly manifest.

A good part of me is leery of love
I don't want to be intoxicated
An obsession is hard to get rid of
Sooner or later I'll be deflated
I can go to the park and watch the sky
I will slow my mind and listen to birds
In the distance I can see a crane fly
And I'm not wasting any time on words
The birds will come and then the birds will go
The clouds and sun are constantly moving
The breeze in the trees does ebb and flow
The rabbits and the squirrels are scampering
My adoration becomes a plaything
I'm not hearing or seeing anything.

My obsession with
her overlays the breeze
in the trees — and the
crane flying — I don't see when
the crane is disappearing.

I haven't lived so long without seeing
That people get crazy involved in love
It's quite common to be fantasying
Of fitting together like hand in glove
But there is a certain reality
That one partner will become dominant
That one possesses the lock and the key
When the passion becomes less prominent
There has to be compatibility
And a forgoing of competition
There's hard work in responsibility
We would need a worthy compensation
When the romantic feeling drains away
We would live with each other every day.

It takes a while for
a real person to emerge
out from under the
fantasy and then how would
reality manifest?

The breeze in the leaves is inspiring
As the clouds are sometimes dimming the light
Simple observation is reviving
The clouds have dispersed and the sky is bright
I'm not really unhappy on my own
What I do with my time I can decide
I'm not going to be using my phone
I'm going to let this relationship slide
The vibrant sky is glorious today
I am watching as the birds come and go
I am happy this Memorial Day
No one is working and I can go slow
I can play with words and think as I please
And I don't have to let myself be teased.

I don't even know
whether her interest in me
goes beyond idle
curiosity and is
only a passing fancy.

The early sonneteers wrote about love
I've followed tradition and played my part
Is my emotion genuine? Sort of
But over the years I've guarded my heart
Love is worthy — love is necessary
Without loving we wouldn't populate
But I wonder what is best for Barry
Love takes more push than I can generate
This afternoon I'll ride my bicycle
The weather is going to be glorious
Looking forward makes me excitable
Pedaling freely is luxurious
For several days I've played Romeo
But my part was only a cameo.

The peonies are
budding with their glorious
superfluity
of lushness as their heavy
blossoms are bending their stems.

One of the ways to mark the progress of
The seasons for me is to come to my
Desk and to note how high the sun is in
The morning and in June there are mornings

When the room is illuminated and
I wear a straw hat with a wide brim to
Shield my eyes so that I can see the screen and
Compose addled poetry and there is

Also the day at the grocery store
When I see in the produce area
The widest bin which I recognize can
Only mean that the watermelons have

Arrived which gives me a treat after I
Ride my bicycle in the afternoon.

I can do without
the political produce
of California
but it's a happy day when
the watermelons arrive.

Every now and then on the news the word
With images will come of an earthquake
In Pakistan or rural China in
Which the concrete buildings crumble and

Crush the people left inside implying
The peril of those trapped and lingering
Buried in the massive rubble injured
And starving waiting for rescue and I

Watch the news knowing that while I brush my
Teeth in a remote location there is
Catastrophe at the neighborhood school
In the ordinary course of a day

It's hard to digest the reality
That such events are inevitable.

That death comes is
is not the difficulty
but that it comes with
such agonizing force is
fathomless perplexity.

It takes me leg-pumping effort to reach
The highest elevation across the
River on my bicycle and I note
The landmarks on the way and more likely

Than not when ascending the final slope
I see a single stem aspiring to
Be a tree and perching on that stem there
Is a redwing blackbird who notices

Me and every time I pass it chirps once
And flies away and now I expect to
See that bird on that stem recognizing
As I do that we are both creatures of

Habit with me following my circuit
And the bird viewing the world from that stem.

The redwing blackbird
possesses the stem
with a view of a hill
and a field of soybeans.

The air is a theater of action
In June as cottonwood puffs are floating
And demonstrating the buoyancy of
Air and on a long ascending slope on

The way to the Crossing Bridge there is
A swarm of gnats forcing me to tighten
My lips and narrow my eyelids lest I
Be irritated and I am spotting white

And yellow moths fluttering revealing
Their leveraging locomotion and
I have measured my speed with the eerie
Maneuverings of brilliant dragonflies

And I have followed the startled flight of
Numerous birds who weren't expecting me.

Way up
turkey vultures
eagles
glide in
thermals
of air.

The intensity of the brilliant light
Of June is worthy of celebration
As I'm facing the window absorbing
Photons that have collided together

For millions of years before reaching the
Surface of the sun liberated and
Launched as I close my eyes and notice the
Red intensity of the light and feel

The pressure of heat on my face and arms
Coincident with the pulsation of
Blood and the rhythm of my breath and I
Didn't do anything to deserve the

Sensations of life as they are a gift
And marvel worthy of celebration.

It's a natural
progression from the workings
of the sun to the
the breathing of the lungs
and the beating of the heart.

The sky absorbs the violence of a
Jackhammer and dissipates it over
Distance and while sitting in Pioneer
Park overlooking a wide river and

A winding valley southward within the
Vast distance there is always a crow a
Crane or a goose flying and there is
So very much to be seeing and I

Tend not to notice the appearance
Or disappearance of birds and only
Watch them momentarily along with
The ephemeral movement of the clouds and

The ruffling of wind in leaves and the play
Of light and shadow moving on the ground.

I'm not so
intoxicated
with people
as to be blind to
the vast horizon.

It's peculiar that people around
The world entertain an obsession
To conquer the height of Mount Everest
Relying on specialized equipment

Gradually acclimating to the
Tipsy altitudes at base camps risking
Hypoxia ascending in a crazed
Push encountering the death zone with

The starvation of oxygen to the
Brain and lungs and every cell staggering
To summit the ultimate top of the
Planet lingering precariously and

Descending to safety amid the rocks
The snow the winds and the severest cold.

The mountain is
littered with the bodies
of those who thought
the attempt was worth
the risk.

You do know how to take me by surprise
To call me in the middle of the day
You know that you're a delight for my eyes
To dangle yourself so that I obey
I had thought it better to let you go
I don't want the bother of obsession
And I am hesitant — but even so
A part of me longs to take possession
To be the body that takes your body
Of this I'm sure that you're well aware of
With all the passion that I embody
You're coaxing it forth and hinting at love
You are an unscrupulous seductress
Seizing my attention with directness.

You know enough of
my schedule to take the
opportunity
to catch me off my guard and
dazzle me with inducements.

I know you're playing on my sympathy
Praising my receptive intelligence
Relying on my ready empathy
You're expressing yourself with eloquence
You would like me to come and meet with you
You want to know how I live so simply
Won't I come to appraise what we could do?
You are confused and feeling dreadfully
How does one learn to let go of trouble?
You would like me to instruct you — you say
I can see that you're brash and quite subtle
I'd really like to come to you today
But I have chores that I have got to do
So much rigmarole to muddle through.

I know instantly
correcting and editing
syntax and grammar
hunting for hidden typos
will now be more difficult.

You want to know how not to be angry
To rise above your ex's pettiness
To not be fuming — to not be cranky
To escape the feeling of emptiness
Your daddy died of alcoholism
Your ex is a terrible drinker too
Both had narcissistic egoism
Which you ignored but really knew was true
You work during the day as a waitress
You're a happy conversationalist
And people are clueless of your distress
But the urge to chatter you can't resist
Men at work are always hitting on you
They press their luck to see what they can do.

Both your ex and your
daddy used intelligence
to be successful
providing opulent homes
in sumptuous neighborhoods.

There is some cruelty in your husband
He is disparaging and calls you names
Which is what you can no longer withstand
In response you do exactly the same
To be cutting in your comments offhand
It's easy to be critical and blame
Usually to gain the upper hand
It becomes a habit that's hard to tame
In divorce you are advancing demands
And now it's a nasty lawyering game
The goal is to gain a judge's command
There is property to righteously claim
For marriage to end like this is a shame
You are resisting an impulse to maim.

He can keep the house
in the swanky neighborhood
but he's got to sell
the boat and pay every month
a hefty spousal support.

There's more drama here than I am used to
My divorce went without complexity
Such bitterness we didn't resort to
I don't see my ex as an enemy
I guess such wild passion becomes a stew
And perhaps it's mixed up with jealousy
With so much history to muddle through
With battles continuing endlessly
And what on earth am I supposed to do
With emotion expressed desperately?
And what trouble am I getting into?
He is arrogant — she is comely
She is beautiful and he has money
He is dogmatic and she is plucky.

Were they made for each other?
To battle with one another?
To squabble and fight
Trading words that bite
Passionately together?

Not getting angry isn't so easy
I had to give up my way of thinking
To let go of victim mentality
And to stop my alcoholic drinking
You can't make a change temporarily
How does one do it without backsliding?
I had to be crushed fundamentally
Such experience isn't appealing
Hitting bottom is a necessity
Otherwise any progress is fleeting
Now I practice in a community
Communication is empowering
I need new power to grow into
A power to give my frustrations to.

The practice becomes
"Let go or be dragged."

Apparently there are some painful pleasures
Where couples come to trouble each other
Subjecting themselves to endless pressure
Jealously squabbling with one another
I wonder what she is seeing in me
Attending and speaking so carefully
Carelessly placing her hand on my knee
Moving in closely quite casually
I know what's happening — I really do
As I notice her eyes are powder blue
Such an intoxicating point of view
I will see what she wants and muddle through
Her fetching presence is tantalizing
Her voice and her words are hypnotizing.

Her curves are tantalizing
Her voice is hypnotizing
But I am careful
And I'm respectful
While she is appetizing.

You know I'm captivated by your charms
And that being with you makes me happy
How could conversing come to any harm?
We are both so fluent and word-savvy
It's not necessary to squabble and fight
I have learned how to live quite peacefully
I don't have trouble sleeping overnight
I've avoided worry successfully
The tricks of detachment I can show you
How to absorb the sunlight — how to breathe
The peace of the *dharma* I can give you
I could navigate with you if you please
You could let go of all your agitation
We could enlighten your cogitation.

Your ex knows how to
manipulate to coerce
you and to push your
buttons befuddling and
destroying your happiness.

The mind operates precariously
What we think about we give power to
Our thoughts happen so precipitously
What we think about we give ourselves to
I have governed myself deceitfully
Supposing I'm controlling what I do
Passion with peace exists uneasily
Sometimes my emotions are torn in two
I aspire to live and love gracefully
And you are showing me that you do too
To think and behave harmoniously
I'm happy to get together with you
To express and to listen equally
I've not had satisfaction recently.

I'm wondering how
such a lovely woman as
yourself could be so
taken in with a person
so unsuited to yourself?

"I was captured by his virility" —
She says — "by his aggression and his looks
His professional capability
Though I knew he was a bit of a crook
But now his behavior has gotten worse
Becoming no more than a drunken louse
There's a quality to him that's perverse
He'd rather have me shut inside the house
I see you operate differently
That you're authentically compassionate
Which is kind of rare — incidentally
And that your words are strangely resonant
I am coming to see that intelligence
Expresses an attractive elegance.

"I don't think you know
the influence of your words
I am curious
how it is you became so
intuitive?" she asks me.

I'm walking about in a happy daze
So satisfied and anticipating
My daydreaming has been a little crazed
Experience is intoxicating
And my meditation is going well
Sitting not moving for forty minutes
Absolutely no problem sitting still
I practice to keep cerebral fitness
I'm doing my editing well enough
Sometimes I am losing my train of thought
Philosophical stuff is kind of tough
Doing the business is an afterthought
In truth I'm reliving my night with her
Ordinary activities are blurred.

I am a nerd who
astonishingly caught a
delightful fish and
now the world is appearing
surprisingly different.

I'm really confused and somewhat put off
So why isn't she answering my calls?
It appears suddenly she's cut me off
Didn't expect to encounter a wall
I do remember reminding myself
Intoxication ends in depression
My sad situation speaks for itself
I guess I'm not done with learning lessons
I've got to decide what I'm going to do
I imagine myself being resolute
Maybe I did something — made a miscue?
Can't stop thinking about her attributes
I'm not going to fret — I'm not going to call
I'm not going to do anything at all.

The Chinese poet
Cold Mountain left the city
kicked off the red dirt
of civilization and
lived with mountains and rivers.

Within two weeks of June the white roses
With a tinge of pink on my patio
And the lushly pink peonies in my
Yard are blooming as the blaze of the

Sun is strengthening as the seasonal
Orbit of the earth about the sun is
Approaching the point of summer solstice
Extending the length of daylight to its

Apogee as roses and peonies
Coincide at my humble abode with
The direction of the solar system
And it happens that the ritual of

My noticing this happy occurrence
Is worthy of quiet celebration.

The cottonwood on
the corner of my yard
is deploying its
array of fully unfolded
leaves absorbing the sunlight.

In a week of afternoons of 90-
Degree Fahrenheit heat I am every
Day ascending the furthest slope with the
Highest elevation of my circuit

On my bicycle on the lookout for
The chirping redwing blackbird who has been
Perching habitually on a stem
And I'm noticing its absence as it's

Apparent that the blaze of the sun is
Too much for the bird and I agree as
I couldn't bear sitting in this shadeless
Heat either but I also notice the

Three-foot stem by the road is a baby
Cottonwood displaying distinctive leaves.

How many of the
numerous aspiring
baby cottonwoods
so clustered together will
escape the county mower?

On a cloudless morning at Pioneer
Park during our gathering while we are
Lounging within lawn chairs discussing a
Way of living apart from addictions

Fran is informing me of the warblers
She is hearing the red-eyed vireo
Olive green above and clean white below
With tail feathers of a green-yellow wash

And the American redstart the males
Black with orange patches and the females
Gray and olive with yellow patches — and
The birds are invisible concealed by

Foliage but their singing is lively
And punctuating our conversation.

Beyond addictions
there are invisible song
birds to be on the
lookout for brightening an
otherwise bland existence.

My thoughts are whirling in captivity
I can't help wondering what you're doing
I feel the lure of compulsivity
As my mind is busy speculating
I am confused within uncertainty
Weighing each of our words — analyzing
Do you control me surreptitiously?
Your motivations are mystifying
I did enjoy you unabashedly
Now your sudden absence is perplexing
What's with this unavailability?
My ignorance is disorienting
Don't know why you're not returning my calls
Suddenly you've erected a brick wall.

My ignorance and
confusion manifests in
scenarios on
top of scenarios that
only inspire longing.

You are a shadow companion to me
Everywhere I go I'm thinking of you
We had such an engaging repartee
Not many women banter as you do
Your words your beauty come along with me
You're an added dimension in my head
I've become a Romeo wannabe
I did have a hint of trouble ahead
I think I'm in love with being in love
I'm using you to hypnotize myself
It's the idea of loving I love
I'm pulling a mighty trick on myself
I'm stuck right now and don't know what to do
My head is busy imagining you.

Infatuation
is a gas transporting me
into whimsical
departures destinations
of happy permutations.

I don't have to be encumbered with you
Comport yourself exactly as you please
You are much more controlling than I knew
You are a voluptuous tricky tease
I am going to go about my business
I have many important things to do
Love is disorienting dizziness
There's more to do than to think about you
I do have my bicycle and my cat
And I can look at my cottonwood tree
You are no more trouble than summer gnats
You are not getting me to bend a knee
Our meeting wasn't serendipity
You've only taken my serenity.

I do want liberation
I enjoyed our flirtation
I not going to fret
Do you want to bet?
I don't want a fixation.

The sun has been burning so brilliantly
The roots of the growing grass are busy
There's no reason to mope despondently
To befuddle myself and become lazy
I just bought a bicycle computer
I can track my time and average speed
To discipline myself and go faster
It takes method and practice to succeed
Where you are doesn't matter much to me
I've got plenty to occupy my time
And what you're doing doesn't concern me
I think maybe I will compose some rhymes
I'm perfectly free to do as I please
Why should I bother with ticks gnats and fleas?

The world is still rotating
The hardy grass is growing
There are things to do
And places to go
There's no need to be moping.

You won't return my calls — I don't know why
I don't think I can do anything more
Probably it's better to say goodbye
It is beyond me to open your door
From now on I know what has to be done
I need to upend and guard my thinking
The excitement I felt can't be undone
You are even disturbing my sleeping
I have to stop when thinking about you
And instantly think about something else
I've got to come up with tricks that will do
I want to think about anything else
Perhaps I can tinker with poetry
And turn my attention to clarity.

Words are always enticing
Composing is inviting
I don't have to lie
I look at the sky
Dragonflies are beguiling.

So differently from my phone which dazzles
My eyes with gaudy and harsh vibrations
When I gaze at the immensity of
Of the sky filled with the ephemeral

And the soothing quality of the clouds
Moving so gradually that one must
Watch attentively and calmly to see
Motion I know that I can dissipate

Disturbance with simple observation
And today amid the towering clouds
I am catching sight of the tiniest
Silhouette of a bird so high up that

I wonder what it's doing so far above
The earth and then it dissolves in the air.

Clouds do express
such ephemeral landscapes
shadowy valleys
and sunlit mountainous peaks
slowly metamorphizing.

In Pioneer Park while leaning back in
My lawn chair and noticing the fully
Grown maple and oak leaves that have now lost
Their sheen of spring brightness I also see

At the edge of my short pants and at the
Ends of the sleeves of my T-shirt there is
A demarcation visible between
The palest of my skin untouched by the

Rays of the sun and a new eminence
Of browning skin which is a token of
The energy of sunlight gracing my
Body during my bicycle rides

About the ups and downs of the river
Valley — and I feel exhilarated.

I imagine my
body as a marshmallow
browning in the fire
of effervescent sunlight
approaching its peak brilliance.

Once the scorching temps relent and summer
Heat returns to milder degrees there are
Cooler interludes in the morning when
The air is suffused and saturated

With the brilliant light of the season and
It's a pleasure to close my eyes facing
The sun and to immerse my consciousness
Within the flushed radiance about my

Face and to see the red quality
Of the light filtered by my eyelids
And I realize that I have waited
A very long time for the pleasures of

Summer to return — to be at my ease
Cavorting in skimpy shorts and T-shirts.

To enjoy the scent
of the white roses on my
patio I have
to immerse my nose in the
petals and inhale deeply.

They aren't as classically beautiful as
The roses but the innumerable
Blooms of white clover are here replacing
The flowering of the dandelions

And creeping charlie and I see monarch
Butterflies and the yellow and white moths
And the dragonflies and fruit flies and
The bumblebees as the permutations

Of summer are coming about again
And I don't mind doing the chores of the
Yard pacing behind the mower once a
Week around the patio apple

Trees the lilac bushes the cottonwood
And I finish in front beside the two pines.

The glare of the sun
is arduous on the hill
and I look forward
to the shady cottonwood
on the northwest corner.

I remember
a woman's
powder blue eyes
and her hand
on my knee.

—*Tekkan*

Everyday Mind XXII

Cloudless morning sky
warms gradually —
some of the white roses
are already wilting.

My roses bloom when summer arrives
Sunny mornings in June are often cool
When the sun and the roses harmonize
That the roses don't last long is the rule
Year after year my rosebushes blossom
They are mostly white with a tinge of pink
That the sky is cloudless happens often
The mild weather and roses are in sync
I do forget the rose's sweet perfume
I have to be close and inhale deeply
The scent is a cynosure of the bloom
It's the rule that roses appear briefly
Each single blossom is ephemeral
The joy of beauty is perennial.

When clouds are absent
when mornings are often cool
the sky is filled with
immeasurable sunlight
that just happens to be blue.

A week before I didn't know my speed
I was just estimating my mileage
Without a grasp of my average speed
I couldn't make use of such knowledge
But as soon as I go fast I can tell
Whether I am doing the same — or better
Now I know what I'm doing very well
Thanks to my new bicycle computer
This little gadget on my handlebars
Is changing my ideas of biking
I know exactly how fast and how far
I'm going and whether I'm improving
But the wind is a pivotal player
An unpredictable force of nature.

Now I'm a greyhound
measuring the minutes and
the distance from
one landmark to the next
from one day to another.

Of all the things going on in a day
Some things are worthy of celebration
Even if I'm having an awful day
Some elements are worth recognition
I don't come to writing casually
I'd like to see what's going to effervesce
And to leverage curiosity
So perceptions and words may coalesce
I give myself to what I attend to
Writing focuses my sincerity
It adds significance to what I do
One of the benefits is clarity
I'd like to be as light as a feather
But tough enough for all kinds of weather.

Crossing boundaries
of what happens and how I
respond I would like
to dissolve who I think I
am and be spontaneous.

Imagine being a fish in summer
Acclimated to persisting current
Would you be sensitive to bright colors?
How often would you resist the current?
Would you be aware of what water is?
Or have an idea of the river?
Would the surface be a strange kind of fizz?
Would other fish be flashes of silver?
Would you know that the river is narrow?
What would you think of the river's surface?
Would you happily wiggle your torso?
Would you recognize your tail's service?
How much of a change would come in winter?
Would you ever have to deal with splinters?

Imagine the shock
of the sudden grasp of an
eagle's sharp talons —
the wrenching departure
from a comfy dimension.

Do you think the trees remember last year?
Does the sky have a hint of memory?
Somehow all of the elements cohere
Life is woven together cleverly
We're growing on a mysterious sphere
This moment goes on interminably
Some of my memories are very dear
But over time they become fantasy
What I'm remembering is a veneer
Memory continues tediously
My eyes and nose and tongue and skin and ears
Are open to life continuously
Experience sometimes becomes severe
I hope I can manage to be sincere.

Am I choosing to
recall as I do or is
remembering a
happening continuing
itself — independently?

When riding my bicycle I am free
I am not compelled to be productive
There are the birds and dragonflies to see
The bright panorama is seductive
The wind's a potent force of contention
The more that I push the more it resists
But even so I do find my traction
Finding a suitable pace — I persist
I don't have to go fast — but I like to
No one is compelling my exhaustion
I expend myself because I want to
With a healthy urge for satisfaction
There's a purity of strength in motion
That balances disturbing emotion.

I tend to measure
my speed against the other
riders that I come
across in a curious
urge of compulsivity.

I don't want the need to feel important
Because then I am measuring myself
And I am seeking others' endorsements
And will be busy promoting myself
Also I have a yearning to be loved
To be comprehensively understood
To comport with someone like hand in glove
Savoring companionship would be good
I am wondering from where does love come?
I think love already resides in me
But my capacity is kind of numb
With too much disturbance to set it free
Love is always there waiting for income
I have to be ready to let it outcome.

Perhaps love is
a dexterous hand
ready to engage with
the earth and people
and I am the glove.

Books can be stuck describing what happened
It need not be necessarily so
I imagine a book without an end
That captures the present and helps it grow
Because miracles are happening now
The seasons repeat again and again
Life gets increasingly burdened somehow
Surprising disappointments are a drain
But there's no ending to this moment now
I can't comprehend all that's happening
It's all simultaneous anyhow
I'm trying to get good at balancing
Can I affix words to liberation?
Don't know — but it is my aspiration.

This moment goes
on and on and all
that goes along with it
is incomprehensible
until now.

Morning is drenched in the summer sunlight
Only a few clouds are drifting southward
The whole expansive river is alight
I'm trying to capture its life with words
The heat of the sun envelops my skin
A million leaves are reflecting the light
And the clouds and the river are akin
Gentle motion is concealing their might
How can one capture this moment now?
It is the point of creativity
Numberless species are living somehow
Emerging beings in activity
There's too much going on to pigeonhole
My viewpoint is only a buttonhole.

In this happenstance
moment the river and the
wisps of the clouds are
progressing gradually
majestically southward.

I'm not going to think about her — not now
Yes — she is beautifully intelligent
I can't get ahold of her anyhow
And I'm wary of her temperament
I'm not naïve with people anymore
The way she hooked me was remarkable
With no explanation she closed the door
And she has made herself unreachable
It's not good to dwell on her lovely eyes
So piercingly intent and powder blue
I really don't think that she told me lies
After all there is nothing I can do
If I let myself go — then I'm to blame
I'm not going to be a moth drawn to flame.

Certainly she has
a most bodacious body
with such fetching curves
but I'm beyond those baubles
with important things to do.

A girlfriend would be inconvenient
I would have to live so differently
Of course there would be our disagreements
When I'd rather act independently
We would be spending evenings on the phone
Going over what happened every day
I'd have to develop a firm backbone
To get at least a portion of my way
And I would have to rearrange my house
She would be over here some of the time
It would almost be like having a spouse
Which would be bodacious part of the time
If only desire could be controlled
But it can't — it just multiplies eightfold.

I'm safely ensconced
in my abode with only
the solicitous
attention of my rowdy
male cat for entertainment.

Sometimes I wake before I intend to
And I'm lying in bed ruminating
I'd like to sleep but I'm unable to
While my head is busy cogitating
Then I'm vulnerable and defenseless
I don't have thinking — the thinking has me
I'm exhausted but my mind is restless
I'm not present — I'm stuck in memory
My life appears as a hall of mirrors
Each reflection is grossly distorted
I am masculine and I don't shed tears
I keep my emotions closely guarded
Relaxation is a wonderful gift
Learning to relax is a handy trick.

I can adopt the
lotus posture before dawn
straightening my back
folding legs over under
breathing and quieting.

It's been so dry that the grass quit growing
With only occasional scraps of clouds
Mostly from the south the wind's been blowing
And blowing on the hills the wind is loud
I wouldn't notice if I weren't riding
The pressure of wind is manageable
Maneuvering in wind is like dancing
Finding the perfect pace is possible
There's joy in motion on my bicycle
There's nothing between me and everything
Perceptions are vibrantly physical
Rushing inside the wind is exciting
I push myself approaching exhaustion
I relax achieving satisfaction.

When the wind pushes
me from behind the air is
quiet and I move
precipitously until
I turn and face its roaring.

The lift part of the bridge is in motion
And pedestrians wait at a closed gate
We riders too wait in position
The gate releases — I become the bait
Going first I leave him following me
Gliding smoothly through the crowd of people
Starting in the right climbing gear is key
I rise and dance lightly on my pedals
I've raced up this hill many times before
But usually I ascend alone
Climbing this hill is what I'm training for
I've made the slope a competitive zone
Near the top I shift to a faster gear
I don't suppose he is anywhere near.

Turning a corner
I glance behind to check for
him seeing him a
little ways behind as I
shift again increasing speed.

You surprised me again by coming here
Walking into my office with coffee
I've not thought about you — you disappeared
I did not forget about your body
You didn't bring the cups — you brought the pot
You are not a person to go halfway
When you do drink coffee you drink a lot
Doing a kind of coffee pot sashay
You're typically brash unconsciously cute
It appears that you've just got out of bed
Your breasts are looking like bulging grapefruits
For me not to see I'd have to be dead
It takes me a while to know what to say
This doesn't happen every other day.

I'm discombobulated
And inarticulated
My tongue is too slow
So my words don't flow
But I'm also elated.

You have certainly come animated
All you can do is to talk about Bruce
Just what I would have anticipated
Your soon-to-be ex is a complete louse
I say it's not worth getting agitated
And I'd like to talk about anything else
Now the way forward is indicated
He can sell the damn boat and keep the house
The divorce decree will be stipulated
You won't have to live with a drunken spouse
Aren't you happy to be liberated?
You're lucky to have gotten a townhouse
At least now I know where you're located
I don't understand why you're frustrated.

Put up with the frustration
Just do the mediation
Let the lawyers work
Don't go so berserk
You'll get your compensation.

I don't mind you coming into my life
Bursting suddenly into my office
I am not beholden to my ex-wife
And I don't want to appear standoffish
But I have questions — what happened to you?
And why did you stop returning my calls?
I wanted to talk but what could I do?
It was like you erected a brick wall
I don't know about your soon-to-be ex
From what you say he's not a nice person
It seems he has a scornful intellect
Your relationship now is going to worsen
I must say that I don't care about him
And the chances of Bruce changing are slim.

So what if he wants the boat?
Who cares if it even floats?
He may be swimming
With other women
But who cares if he's a goat?

It's just that I've been conflicted — she says —
My mind's been racing and I've been upset
And I get entangled in what he does
I have been lost in a crabby mindset
And I am not even charging my phone
I'm sorry that I've caused you to worry
But I'm spending most of my time alone
Please — could you find a way to forgive me?
I've missed your company and your kind words
Of all my friends — you — best — understand me
I've been so angry and also quite bored
I believe that you know how to help me
So — Barry — I don't know what I would do
Without a compassionate man like you.

I've had to move all my stuff
And every day has been rough
I have been weary
And also teary
I've already had enough.

She's given me a lot to think about
Can she truly not be charging her phone?
Divorce does make sensitive people pout
And I'm relieved that she says she's alone
Of all her friends I best understand her
And she chose to burst in on me today
I know the trials of divorce are severe
Few of us can really expect fair play
I don't like being left in the dark
I'm happy to be in contact again
We didn't say any unkind remarks
And perhaps both of us are under strain
I do suspect she knows what she's doing
I will not put up with any lying.

Before I had no answers
And couldn't make advances
I was damn lonely
My days were stony
I didn't like my chances.

This obsession over this girl is like
A fizzle in my consciousness skewing
My perspective and limiting what I
Could be experiencing even though

I'm not a novice in love and am well
Apprised of how such intoxication
Dissipates revealing imbalances
And disharmonies perhaps fixable

With sincere efforts towards empathy but
Probably not as I can attest with
Years of disappointment and so I ask
What am I doing indulging such an

Infatuation thereby foregoing
Uncluttered unburdened liberation?

With the mission of
obtaining kitty litter
and mouthwash walking
in Walmart's parking lot I
see the swallows have returned.

When asked how liberation appears a
Zen master said it's like everyday life
Except one is floating two inches off
Of the ground as I remembered in the

Parking lot of Walmart seeing a flight
Of swallows acrobatically swooping
And darting about the entrance dancing
In air having returned for the summer

From their migration south for a reason
That is known only to them they frolic
Around a strip mall in Minnesota
Showing that mundane human existence

Isn't separated from the vast and
Interwoven workings of the cosmos.

The swallows may be
looking down upon Walmart
on occasion but
not in condescension as
they are not at all snobs.

It's obvious what romantic love is
When I am dressed up in my clip-on shoes
And sleek fabric jersey slicing through the
Wind on my bicycle pedaling with

A practiced cadence through the countryside
For an hour into my ride when I come
To the cynosure and the ultimate
Test of my ride ascending the steep slope

To Holton when I rise from my seat and
Dance on the pedals and at apparent
Ease at first but somewhere along the way
I begin to strain and to gasp for breath

With every kick of the pedals as my
Entire consciousness narrows to a point.

The focused effort
of consciousness narrows
with the strain of a
lusting eliminating
the splendiferous cosmos.

I'm seeing monarch butterflies thinking
Maybe these are those that migrated from
Mexico or perhaps they are the next
Generation and I see them on the

Bike beating the air fluttering as they
Do in their peculiar fashion as I'm
Pumping my legs on a slope straining with
Effort in my breathing lungs and beating

Heart and yet my sight is stable and not
Like the butterflies that must be viewing
The world in a jerky sequence of ups
And downs and I'm guessing that they are not

Queasy with air sickness nor do they have
Vertigo as I suspect that I would.

The monarchs and I
are rotating with the earth
orbiting the sun
orbiting the Milky Way
expanding from the Big Bang.

I wasted my time in conversation
Yesterday aware of passing minutes
Considering how long I would stay with
Friends I haven't been able to meet with

For a year face to face because of the
Pandemic thinking soon I would go to
Do writing until I realized how
Stupid I was not to appreciate

Genuine friendship reunited in
The happy exchange of shared views making
The difference between the endurance
Of or the curious exploration

Of life wherein allies pique my thoughts and
Embolden me within difficult days.

Yesterday I did
not get to my writing
but instead the weight
of isolation lifted
in connection with friends.

In my daily passage of it on my
Bicycle I imagine the scope of
A field of soybeans of advances
Of knowledge over millennia and

Of the application of satellite
Analysis of the soil and of the net
Of regulations ruling each of the
Taxable acres and of the rise of

Corporate farms replacing family
Farms with the management of sowing and
Harvesting feeding international
Markets and affecting diplomatic

Relationships and worldwide appetites
Harnessing the sun the soil and water.

The surface of the
earth is continuing to
undulate over
millennia rising up
with mountains and eroding.

I assume Kitcat is chasing a bug
Bunching up the rug by the door but he's
Blocking something with his paws again and
Again and he's pouching and springing and

His tail is whipping and balancing his
Body and then I see the pitiful
Little black mouse frantically turning with
Kitcat inescapably hovering

Over him as they go thudding down the
Stairs to the basement as I go about
The business of changing the water in
His water dishes and refilling the

Container with cat food while listening
To commotion until quiet returns.

I rescue the third
dazed mouse with an injured
leg picking it up
with a towel and putting it
on the patio outside.

I think that I know what I'm doing but
Life has a way of revealing many
Delusions as I returned after a
Two-year absence to the dentist's office

For the scraping away of plaque and a
Polishing and for two types of X-rays
Involving unforeseen gadgets with the
Usual discomfort along with the

Attention of a female hygienist which
I like but this time she pronounced the term
"General recession" which the dentist
Explains means that my gums are receding

From my teeth and exposing some of the roots
And "no" the gums will not grow back again.

Three times a day when
using my electric tooth
brush it appears that
I've been applying too much
pressure which I now regret.

It's easy to be hypnotized by the
Edges of things into emphasizing
My separation within my skin from
The carnival of events happening

Continually around me such as
With the lacerating suddenness of
A bald eagle flying and clutching a
Fish in its talons or with the motion

Of a willow tree on a summer day
While I am trying to realize that
Wherever I am looking there isn't
A separation between events but

Only a flowing of happenings in
All directions like ripples of water.

I can't help making
distinctive demarcations
between happenings
one after another but
choosing is arbitrary.

My daughter Jocelyn is using the
White of primer to paint on white fabric
Reviving photographic images
Snapped by her Japanese great-grandfather

When he was an Imperial soldier
In on the conquest of China eighty
Years ago capturing the instant when
A young troop while standing was reading the

Similar ink writings between China
And Japan on a magazine cover
And if I look at the painting today
From one angle the image is gray but

If I look from the opposite view it's
A distinctly white and ghostly image.

Do you suppose in
the instant of the photo
the soldier could have
imagined eighty years on
This result of the photo?

Brushing before dawn used to be the high
Point of the day for us when I would turn
Him on his back and brush from beneath his
Chin to tail and then I'd brush his back and face

After which we'd have a contest of wills
And dexterity when he'd flip himself
To his back and I'd slap him with both my
Hands all over him as he tried to bite

My fingers which he sometimes did and he
Would often yowl during the contest but
One day he decided not to play the
Game anymore and immediately

After the brushing he left me sitting
Uselessly on the floor watching him leaving.

It dawned on me that
my elusive slapping may
have caused frustration
to accumulate until
Kitcat decided to quit.

I would like to celebrate the humble
Cucumber that I buy in the produce
Part of the grocery store to adorn
My toasted ham and cheese sandwich every

Lunch because although its taste is quite bland
It provides my consciousness with the salve
That I am eating my vegetables
And it's amazing the number of days

Through which I can consume but a single
Cucumber by slicing judicially
Thinly and even the procedure of
Cutting a cucumber brings me a tinge

Of satisfaction as it's civilized
Easy and not unpleasant to gaze on.

I am biased to
believe a cucumber
is not a fruit but
a vegetable because
I do need to eat veggies.

o to be archy the poet who died
and was born again in the body of
a cockroach laboring ceaselessly to
express himself by jumping off of the

frame of a typewriter headfirst to strike
a key to make a letter composing
in a day of hard labor a simple
short poem without the benefit of

capital letters because he couldn't
work the shift key and yet during the night
freddy the rat another poet would
come and eat the paper destroying the

earthly record of archy's prodigious
efforts reducing life to misery.

don marquis the
journalist created the
idea of the
unfortunate poet in
imitation of himself.

Cobwebs in the corner of the windows
And motes of dust floating in the air and
A wasp bobbing and momentarily
Resting on a leafy hedge outside of

The window amid the intense light of
The summer sun ascending to a good
Height in the morning perhaps leads one to
believe nothing much is going on but

No as the heat is warming my skin to
The verge of sweat and I look under
The brim of a straw hat with a weave of
Gaps through which the sun sparkles but also

Somewhat shields my eyes from the glare I am
Liberated enough to be relaxed.

One doesn't need a
reason for relaxing but
being able to
in vexing circumstances
is a propitious ploy.

Sometimes I'd rather not compose poems
Of significance as I would have to
Summon a serious attitude which
I have to do often enough so now

I will recount the saga of buttering
Two slices of toast improving them with
A layering of ham and cheese to be
Superimposed with cucumber which I

Slice with loving care after which I make
My way to the couch to settle myself
Upon to watch the *Tour de France* while I
Inattentively move to take a bite

But then my fingers fumble and a slice
Of the cucumber drops and vanishes.

I couldn't find it
anywhere until I saw
the dust-bespotted
slice of cucumber had rolled
a good way across the room.

I do like to talk to you everyday
And it's easy to be in touch by phone
It's important for me to have my say
As I think about you when I'm alone
As soon as I'm awake I love to call
And now you're answering every morning
It was hard for me when you put up your wall
But now I'm excited that we're talking
At 5 a.m. I'm calling your number
While lying in bed I'm talking to you
Our conversation allays my hunger
I yearn to talk and it seems you do too
Every morning we're having pillow talk
Sometimes I wake early and watch the clock.

Your idea to
talk on the phone at 5
a.m. before dawn
is a wonderful way to
start my day — thinking of you.

So with new habits I have to adapt
I am delaying my meditation
And rejiggering my schedule in fact
Causing more than a little disruption
I love to be able to interact
Stimulated by our conversation
Your voice is having a touching impact
Feeding an urge for anticipation
I am soaking up your daily doings
Getting to know your intimate habits
Becoming familiar with your thinking
Appreciating your verbal talents
And after our predawn conversation
I am digesting new information.

Pillow talk
predawn intimacy
is becoming the
cynosure
of my days.

You don't trust Bruce and he owes you money
You still share an account at Bremer Bank
There's a circumstance that's kind of funny
An opportunity to play a prank
He has been on a list for twenty years
To be a member of the country club
Now his number is up — his way is clear
He has $4,000 to pay up
He thinks that he can be a golfing fool
All he has to do is to pay the fee
He's clearly forgotten you know the rules
And you intend to withdraw that money
When he writes a check he will be surprised
His cherished wish will have to be revised.

The mediators
haven't decided on the
dispursal of funds
so he's not entitled to
claim his golfing membership.

Your Daddy was a smart entrepreneur
And he once owned a lumber company
And he was a successful inventor
With a patent earning lots of money
He wasn't a very faithful husband
And put your mother through enormous grief
He's reminding me of your ex-husband
There's a pattern here — that is my belief
Your Daddy drank a lot of alcohol
Normal behavior in your family
He would go to bars and get into brawls
And he died before the age of fifty
Your family did enjoy prosperity
Then suddenly you lived in poverty.

It's astounding how
drinking's a thread woven
through generations
of your family — also
affecting your brother's life.

You remember a good friend from childhood
You were swimming together at the beach
She wore a tight bathing suit with a hood
The fabric was so very tightly stretched
She was protruding and looking silly
And you couldn't stop yourself from laughing
She had chubby cheeks and a big belly
It was obvious you hurt her feelings
And you do remember feeling guilty
But the damage had already been done
You wavered between laughter and pity
While your outburst kind of ruined the fun
There's so much trauma — even from grade school
Kids can be unintentionally cruel.

You told your Dad the
story afterward because
you did feel guilty
but in the telling the two
of you couldn't stop laughing.

Your family was happy for a while
Until about your junior high school age
Your Dad dying suddenly was a trial
Your Mom struggled to make a living wage
She was forced to work a couple of jobs
There was persisting insecurity
But she did persevere against the odds
Hardship brought you early maturity
Difficulty marred your adolescence
The loss of your Daddy was a burden
He was such a dominating person
You missed his calming masculine presence
Losing your Dad was a calamity
But your Mom came through for the family.

Your Dad was a rogue
dynamically exciting
and afterward the
quiet absence in the house
was difficult to endure.

In high school you were a popular girl
You dated the football quarterback star
Those years went by in an ecstatic whirl
And I believe they made you who you are
Truthfully you didn't care about him
Your personalities didn't quite fit
He was more often suited to the gym
After graduation you knew you'd split
But you liked getting so much attention
You were talkative — you were sociable
Faux celebrity was your dimension
All this information is notable
I understand your personality
How you formulate rationality.

To me you appear
as a queen of beauty a
little worse for wear
with the slightest tinge of
dissipation about you.

After high school you attended college
At the university in Duluth
You enjoyed learning and gaining knowledge
You met Bruce and comprehended the truth
You understood his cast of character
He was a rogue and a heavy drinker
You guessed that he'd be a good provider
With him you found genuine desire
With him you had what we call chemistry
Your personalities bonded with glue
And should we say that's serendipity?
In the end it didn't work out for you
He makes a sport of disparaging you
He isn't nice — as you already knew.

Sometimes it's a shame
that like attracts like and with
time the qualities
bringing couples together
may end up destroying them.

You left college without graduating
You married and he finished his degree
His job is financially rewarding
And you started having a family
He does electrical engineering
He returned to get a master's degree
Enabling him to begin managing
Which earns an even higher salary
For him you gave up your education
Which now has become a major regret
Being limited is a frustration
Being unsupported is quite a threat
You take so much pride in both of your sons
Raising them is the best thing you've done.

You are counting on
a substantial amount of
spousal support from
the divorce decree which is
entirely justified.

You went to work when your kids entered school
And you really do enjoy waitressing
His disapproval is certainly cruel
Your freedom is beyond his controlling
You have always loved being sociable
And you are being paid to talk all day
Conversing is more than comfortable
Bantering with customers is child's play
You're getting the attention you desire
You have many relationships at work
You've transformed yourself into a server
Having wide social contact is a perk
It irks him that you are cute and friendly
That so many are complimentary.

There is a guy who
every year is buying you
a Christmas tree as
a kind of a fetish which does
tend to make Bruce unhappy.

I have never known such intimacy
My ex and I weren't nearly as fluent
I'm learning details with intricacy
I do not believe this is imprudent
Who would have believed that at 5 a.m.
I'd be talking to a lovely woman?
I'm surprised at how elated I am
I think I'm becoming fully human
New experience is blooming for me
Digesting the world through another's eyes
Conversation is good — and we agree
And communication is best without lies
Every day when I'm getting out of bed
Thoughts of her are occupying my head.

For the rest of the
day I'll be considering
new information
and how differently life
appears from another view.

I had a friend in Hutchinson Kansas
It was my first taste of companionship
With him I knew an easy happiness
I remember our genuine friendship
And fifty years on I don't recall much
But I'm aware of a hole in my heart
So much of my life I've felt out of touch
I am familiar with living apart
It's not been easy to communicate
I've put it down to mismatched chemistry
With people I tend to reach a stalemate
I live with a dose of perplexity
For easy companionship it's a must
For intimacy I have to have trust.

My family moved
from Hutchinson Kansas
to Minnesota
where in Bayport the kids
were nasty and combative.

Playing with words comes easily to me
I like to express what I'm perceiving
When saying what I want I do feel free
Clarifying my thoughts is exciting
With most people there is hesitancy
There are hidden barriers in the way
I've come to keep my distance guardedly
And too often I don't know what to say
Pristine sheets of paper open to me
I can express exactly what I want
The receptive paper and I agree
I've found a reliable confidant
There is a purity in playing with words
And I don't care if I'm sounding absurd.

The presence of the
paper serves as the best of
friends until it may
happen that a flesh and blood
person comes along I hope.

For some reason we can articulate
Conversation comes without an effort
She bandies her phrases and innovates
Our manner of relating does comport
She tells her story and it resonates
She's in a distressing situation
And for her — isolation suffocates
It's better to express the frustration
Perhaps some solutions may percolate
I'm not going to tell her what she should do
While talking — ideas may germinate
And she may grasp what she already knew
Listening carefully can be a game
I really do believe she feels the same.

If she hadn't called
me there was no way that I
would have taken the
initiative to call her —
she is uninhibited.

She understands how attractive she is
I'm astounded that she's talking to me
I know how intoxicating she is
And comprehend that there's no guarantee
I'm weighing implications in her words
Speculating what she feels about me
Nothing she is saying goes unexplored
I feel the sting of insecurity
I want to be cared about — to be loved
With her is that a possibility?
Presently the question is unresolved
The truth will emerge eventually
She is bursting with sexuality
Topping pleasing compatibility.

I don't like being
exposed but I'm already
hooked and excited
so I'm going to keep talking
and see what eventuates.

Suppose you imagine how life could be
Without the burden of inhibitions
From my point of view you're already free
You are able to change your conditions
Which you are doing by talking to me
Not being bound by self-definitions
But don't always expect to be carefree
Don't waste energy in competition
Problems with solutions tend to agree
You're not liking your present position
So envision where you would like to be
Which could be an open proposition
Perhaps judgment day for a divorcee
May well turn out to be a jubilee.

Why drag around
all those old arguments and
bitter memories
when you could be learning the
best lesson — how to relax?

Most of my anguish comes from my thinking
I don't notice what it's doing to me
I'm not supple — I'm only reacting
I would like to use spontaneity
It's a matter of developing poise
Relaxing is a propitious game
Reducing my troubles to background noise
I don't have to struggle argue and blame
So how may I relax when I want to?
Relaxing is a trick that takes practice
Of releasing thinking when I need to
My thoughts are like a prickly cactus
I accept that I may not get my way
I'll do something else on another day.

I rely on a
simple idea of a
power greater than
myself that I partner with —
this power takes care of me.

Relaxing is the hardest trick there is
Because I don't think about doing it
I concentrate on doing my business
Without a success I don't want to quit
But my relationships don't work like that
Especially when involving affections
I'm not good at manipulating that
Compelling people in my direction
I cannot make people care about me
Perhaps lovers grow into each other
I have to relax and to let things be
Somehow companions find one another
Being cheerful is very attractive
It has to be true to be effective.

I practice being
lonely and cheerful at the
same time trusting
wonderful developments
are just around the corner.

Something about me tickles your fancy
We've been conversing now every morning
I'm liking our talk — it makes me happy
Starting the day with you is exciting
We're saying hello right at 5 a.m.
There are always new topics to explore
I don't want to be hungry — but I am
I'm surprised that you're eager — but you are
The hours we're talking are filling my day
They make me ponder for deeper meanings
Afterward I consider what you say
I'm looking to foster new beginnings
Conversing on the phone every morning
Every evening is worth the waiting.

To hear your voice say
my name at 5 a.m. when
most people are still
sleeping has a certain thrill
worth the anticipation.

All relationships are perishable
I think this is something you understand
Not only if you're incompatible
Even with your sincerity on hand
Over time people grow differently
And they come to grate against each other
We all have quirks of personality
So it's good to forgive one another
But relationships don't have to perish
Can you give your partner a gentle touch?
And refrain from imposing your answers?
But who am I to talk so overmuch?
These are questions that I haven't mastered
There is something that's beyond chemistry
A loving patience is a remedy.

Maybe I'm a great
fool to be talking like this
as I'm divorced too
and spending my holidays
as a singularity.

You're angry at the cook for what he said
He accused you of being "such a woman"
It certainly seems that he's a blockhead
You could have said he's a troglodyte man
There's a lot going on at your café
Your friend Sherry is a likeable girl
She can make a new boyfriend every day
From your description she's like a showgirl
No wonder Bruce got so jealous of you
You're enjoying a vibrant social life
And I really have to give you your due
You're more than an ordinary housewife
I do like using the word "cynosure"
I think you possess plenty of allure.

Meanwhile I am all
by my lonely self at the
office going through
essays correcting grammar
redoing faulty syntax.

How lucky we were to find each other
It's so simple to have conversation
To listen and talk to one another
While cultivating our relaxation
I'm curious how your days are going
I'm giving you my eager attention
The littlest details are engaging
Enlivening our daily narration
And I also get to talk about me
And to express all of my hidden thoughts
You're giving me the opportunity
I'm getting to untie my secret knots
You're helping me discover who I am
To say what I think — and not give a damn.

It's only because
you are listening to me
that I have the chance
to express my daily thoughts
that would have been forgotten.

You're saying that Sherry is a real tease
She doesn't care about the men she knows
She doesn't go out of her way to please
Her availability is a pose
These poor guys will do anything for her
Lacking a clue of her indifference
She's turning love into a ligature
Their sincerity makes no difference
You don't appreciate her behavior
You're saying it reflects her bitterness
She's getting back at the guys who've hurt her
She's completely consumed with unhappiness
She's already divorced — three times over
Nothing's worse than a disgruntled lover.

Taking orders at
the café is the perfect
ploy for snaring the
unsuspecting fools who
eagerly keep showing up.

I feel some pressure to make things happen
I'm infatuated with this woman
Emotions kickstart my adrenaline
I want to be her only leading man
But she is talking to plenty of guys
While I'm stuck in my office by myself
With Bruce I'm beginning to empathize
Like him I feel deserted on a shelf
I'm building up the nerve to ask her out
I feel impelled to seize the momentum
I can't be inhibited by my doubts
I've got uncertainty to overcome
I just can't be quiet — I have to move
I've got my masculinity to prove.

The aching yearning
of love forced me to ask her
out on Friday night
and we'll be meeting at a
fancy Chinese restaurant.

I am beginning to feel the weight of
A sickening familiarity
She said yes — giving me more to dream of
This doesn't solve my insecurity
I'm anticipating our coming date
And imagining how she'll dress for me
Excited daydreaming is really great
It has the appearance of being carefree
But now my emotions are invested
I'm starting to yearn for certain results
Because I know nothing is guaranteed
Moderating myself is difficult
I want to see that she cares about me
This harrowing feeling won't let me be.

I'd like to wrench out
my insecurity and
be as casual
and as nonchalant as a
forgetful Lothario.

She does enjoy my sensitivity
Savoring my able conversation
She likes my easy creativity
I think I'm winning her admiration
She says she wants to keep talking to me
It helps to lessen her aggravations
She's feeling a taste of despondency
And experiencing wild gyrations
She's getting divorced and can't let it be
Her future income is a fixation
She does need money to live happily
Her love is worth some remuneration
She's not letting Bruce get off easily
She demands to be treated decently.

I do wish that she
would forget about Bruce as
obviously he's
a bully and a drunk and
how can that be attractive?

There's a paradox in liberation
At least of the type that I am seeking
Trying too hard creates separation
I'd like to give up the habit of grasping
There is the initial desperation
A lingering period of suffering
That's enough to inspire frustration
That culminates in a new beginning
From there what's needed is relaxation
A peace apart from unending striving
Fascination with subtle vibrations
There is patience to be cultivating
I want to surf with my motivations
I would like to balance with emanations.

Romantic love and
political victory
may be delusions
to be grasped only for a
moment before they dissolve.

Our evening together went splendidly
And it ended with a lingering kiss
Leaving me dreaming again hungrily
Thinking of ways that we could coalesce
She wants to keep on talking frequently
And again tomorrow in the morning
Which I'm looking forward to eagerly
To begin the day with our conversing
But something seems a little odd to me
I think I'm noting a little distance
She's parceling affections carefully
I'm getting a sense of some resistance
She is not as open as she could be
So I will play along and wait and see.

Our rendezvous on
the phone as I'm lying
in my bed and she's
sitting up drinking coffee
isn't quite enough for me.

Do people fall in love — and recover?
I wonder why we use the word "falling"
Like jumping out of a plane together
To experience a weightless floating?
This changes my sense of reality
Fixing my attention on a lover
Perhaps it's happening naturally
Involving obstacles to get over
Passion is taking so much attention
I don't want to live like this everyday
It is a constant and stressful tension
Straining to find exciting things to say
And my lingering doubts won't let me be
That perhaps she is only teasing me.

The necessary
details of getting through the
ordinary chores
of my daily life do make
me increasingly weary.

She says on the phone that she enjoys me
She suspects I don't know my influence
That I have an intriguing history
And sometimes my words cast a kind of trance
That I'm not like the other guys she's known
There's depth and breadth that is exceptional
And that when her thoughts won't let her alone
I'm helping her to be more flexible
It's true — each situation is unique
And can be viewed from different angles
There are various solutions to seek
When stubborn attitudes are untangled
But most of all she likes my gentle touch
And she likes my attention very much.

She doesn't know the
influence she's having on
me as I struggle
with my equanimity
and with love's uncertainty.

I choose cyclical over linear
Time putting faith in the rising and the
Setting of the sun and the orbiting
Of the earth around the sun producing

The seasons demonstrating the constant
Arising and disintegration of
Things even as I experience age
And so many of the people I've known

Live only now as a diminishing
Memory surely to vanish with me
But the fact of consciousness is so odd
Why shouldn't we suppose it continues

And rejoice because we don't have to earn
The perpetual beating of our hearts?

Perhaps like winter
death is only a season
of life which bursts its
bonds and blooms again into
youth and curiosity.

The idea that birth and death happen
Only once makes the pivotal moments
Of adolescence and young adulthood
And middle age so much more fretful as

Opportunity must be seized or lost
Forever and then how much weightier
Does remorse become with consequences
And how much sharper are resentments toward

People who get in the way and how much
More fearful does the future appear as
An end is coming as a monstrous void
Liable to create terrors of mind as

Of being buried alive unable
To breathe in suffocating loneliness.

We are just conscious
enough to be forced into
making conceptions
about the passage of time
and about our own demise.

My quiet attention allowed me to
See without the hinderance of stray and
Meaningless repetitive thoughts a crow
Land on the grass and utter its caw in

A guttural manner with its throat and
With its beak and then I noticed it walk
Taking many stiff strides across the grass
Which is a sight I've not seen before and

Its gait on its spindly legs reminded
Me of a portly formally dressed old
Gentleman with his hands in the pockets
Of his suitcoat as he stepped awkwardly

Along perhaps as he was attending
A funeral and casting gloom about.

I suppose
once in a while
a crow needs to
exercise its legs.

None of us has any excuse to be
Bored as we can always give ourselves to
The birds as a grey catbird casts a spell
On me on a video as the bird

Mimics a green-winged teal a Wilson's snipe
A Western kingbird a Western bluebird
A Western meadowhawk a rock hen a
Spotted towhee a red-wing blackbird and

A Pacific tree frog and I didn't
Glean the knowledge of these birds myself through
Years of observation because I could
Rely on the expert from the Cornell

Lab but now it's incumbent on me to
Open my ears and eyes to the marvels.

Perhaps the male grey
catbird is impressing the
female with its fine
repertoire exclaiming — "I
am a bird that gets around."

I like the Buddhist symbology of
The bodhisattva who's enlightened but
Chooses to linger within the world of
Suffering and its gender is pictured

As male or female at different times
And the transcendent being is believed
To be busy with a thousand arms and
Hands interacting and easing the plight

Of those who are burdened regardless of
Whether the hardships are obvious or
Subtle to those who suffer with sorrow
Without knowing the reasons why and who

Feel abandoned because to me it means
There's much more going on than I can know.

Unexplainable
reassurance sometimes comes
when surrendering
the burdensome perspectives
of the past and the future.

My ex-wife comes to my house to get the
Mail that continues to be misaddressed
And she always wants to greet my cat whom
She loves as they had a close connection

And I would often see them in bed with
Him lying on top of her as if he
Owned her but she has been out of the house
For a year and a half and every time

She returns Kitcat is standoffish and
I wonder whether he has forgotten
Her or he's upset that she's abandoned
Him according to his way of thinking

And yesterday after she left again
I saw Kitcat motionless on a chair.

Kitcat can't express
emotions with words and I
don't suppose he
distinguishes feelings but
I suspect that he was sad.

I remember how my mentor used to
Compliment the people he liked with a
Characteristically back-handed phrase
That sounded so odd to me because Cid

A master of poetry was so much
Older coming from a generation
Which invented idioms that have since
Gone out of fashion and are forgotten

And now Cid has passed decades ago and
Lives only as a memory but the
Other day in a dream the phrase he used
Anointing someone as a rebel and

A friend and a fellow traveler came
To me — he was an "offbeat" character.

In the poetry
community Cid is thought
to be among the
beatnik poets which is an
appellation he denied.

R.I.P. Cid Corman

In the process of assembling words
I don't know what I'm doing right away
As I'm starting with the impetus of a
Phrase or of an image that piques my

Curiosity and I know there is
Something within the shallows of my mind
And that I have to linger patiently
On the edge of the inexpressible

As if I were fishing in a Jon boat
And then suddenly while placing one word
Beside another I get a piercing
Insight into what it is I'm trying

To say and the whole point of a poem
Plops into a moment of clarity.

The plop creates
ripples of connections
I could have found
in no other way.

As a novice to the poetry scene
I went to readings to get my bearings
And Mike was a funny and a gritty
And sometimes a bellowing poet worn

With effort and well appreciated
In St. Paul and Minneapolis as
A guy who's been around for decades
Which I didn't know but I did sense that

He was someone who knew his way about
And with some embarrassment I showed him
The seven books that I had self-published
And he expressed mild admiration

On a gloomy winter night and he said
Often poets can't give their stuff away.

Mike Finley dubbed
the king of St. Paul poets
was busy dying
of cancer coming to terms
with an indifferent world.

Viktor Frankl was busy digging a
Ditch in the frozen ground under a gray
Sky on a gray morning dressed in his gray
Concentration camp pajamas yearning

For his wife not knowing where she was
But remembering her nurturing and
Loving encouragement when he was freed
By a perception into the secret

Of the meaning of poetry that the
"Salvation of man is through love in love"
Understanding when one has nothing left
He may yet know bliss if only in a

Moment through the loving contemplation
Within the image of his beloved.

A bird perched
on the pile of dirt
he accumulated
and peered intently
at him.

I do find myself imagining how
I am appearing to the one I love
And I'm guessing what she's thinking somehow
Contemplating the traits that I'm proud of
Replaying words we've spoken together
Taking encouragement in things she's said
Assessing the words that really matter
I could have said something better instead
I've turned her into a mirror of me
And I'm imagining what she's feeling
But I don't know if our passions agree
My distorted image is confusing
I'm lost in a hall of funhouse mirrors
The more I think — they're not getting clearer.

I just know that
I'm trying too hard to make
things happen that are
beyond my control and that
I really have to relax.

I called several times with no response
And sent several text messages too
I'm adopting a pose of nonchalance
While stymied and wondering what to do
I suppose it's my responsibility
To make the first moves and see what happens
While working on my insecurity
I may have to surrender my passion
Girls are like buses — another's coming
It's not a benefit to care so much
Our predawn calls were encouraging
But now once again we are out of touch
I have got to accept the way things are
This crazy situation is bizarre.

With a head-turning
woman like her I'd always
be wondering who
else she is talking to
and I will not live like that.

I am on a quest to discover love
I'm feeling pressure to make things happen
What she's doing I have no control of
While I get these bursts of adrenaline
I am on edge and it's sharp and jagged
And I don't know why she's being aloof
I don't like being purposely ignored
I'm not surprised that I'm not shatterproof
As I search my thoughts for explanations
I struggle with my curiosity
Suffering now for my expectations
I'd like a little reciprocity
I'm a victim of my aspirations
Solitude feels like asphyxiation.

Yeah I know that I'm
putting myself under a
massive amount of
pressure but why the hell is
she choosing not to reply?

Hello my ridiculous gyrations
You're putting me through the wringer today
With unobtainable aspirations
I'll figure this out on another day
I'm better than this — I know my value
I am not going to let you scramble my head
This crazy passion is just a snafu
So I'll think about something else instead
I'm not going to let you agitate me
I know how to meditate and be calm
Practicing serenity is my key
I know your essence — you are a pipe bomb
I'm disbelieving you my demon doubt
On another day I'll figure this out.

The lotus posture
is my dissolving machine
moving energy
along my spine through my limbs
dissipating crazy thoughts.

I know she is a social butterfly
She has plenty of opportunity
I don't know what her absence signifies
I'm not enjoying my passivity
I am going to return to match.com
Female company is available
Loneliness is a fragmentation bomb
Doing nothing isn't acceptable
I've done it before — I know what to do
I'll leave a hundred messages today
There are all these profiles to go through
And I'm certain to get some interplay
Most won't respond — but I really don't care
Nothing is happening if I don't dare.

I'm able to be
indifferent about the
massive numbers of
women online until I
get a glimpse of who they are.

During college I read a short story
About a guy with a beautiful wife
The emotion of the tale was heavy
Showing the cataclysm of his life
His wife began to drift away from him
With a separation of affection
For no reason weightier than a whim
She never gave him an explanation
She just stopped talking and left him alone
When confronted all she did was to weep
At the end of the tale his wife was gone
He had a terrible time trying to sleep
It is odd that she was the one weeping
And yet it was he who wasn't sleeping.

Who knows what really
happened between the couple
and it's possible
important facts were left out
but I feel sorry for him.

I do love listening to Alan Watts
He's a master of ancient Eastern wisdom
He's helping me with my consciousness knots
Feeding my craving for mysticism
The point of his talk is liberation
I listen to him while driving my car
His words propose a cosmic flirtation
On occasion he will reference a star
He says the star and I are related
Our existence depends on each other
Though the connections are complicated
It's true that we are woven together
I am waiting for that bolt of lightning
A change of view that is enlightening.

Alan says the more
I seek for liberation
the further away
I thrust it from me because
it cannot be seized by force.

Alan's temperament is humorous
He jokes about a goose in a bottle
There is a point — he's not gratuitous
The plight of the goose is a boondoggle
So how can we get the goose out alive?
The Zen master is stubbornly silent
There's no solution that we can contrive
It doesn't help to become more strident
The master takes another direction
It seems he's forgotten about the goose
He's even joyful in misdirection
And then he exclaims that the goose got loose
It just happened without explanation
Maybe because of its relaxation?

Alan's tale about
the Zen master and the goose
is reassuring
about liberation and
a lover's befuddlement.

Alan talks about Hindu mythmaking
He dwells upon the game of hide and seek
The Gods are laughing — the Gods are dancing
They hide their faces and then — take a peek
But how does this comport with suffering?
When we squirm and strain to escape our pain?
When the impact of life is confusing?
It's hard to determine what's most humane
Alan talks about the game of our dreams
Soon enough we'd be bored with paradise
Constant happiness is not what it seems
Perhaps our troubles are a kind of spice
We couldn't know happiness without strife
Having hardships gives meaning to a life.

The intensity
the suffering may be too
much to be borne and
yet the game continues on
perhaps to awakening.

The unhindered mind is spontaneous
With thought following thought following thought
And often they are miscellaneous
But my dilemmas come in getting caught
Liberation need not be difficult
As long as I'm not picking and choosing
When I'm yearning for a certain result
And that is when I will be suffering
Then how does one love and also succeed
With desire approaching possession?
Because I'd like to be spreading my seeds
And I'm cultivating a fixation
This girl is dangling just beyond my reach
And I'm so focused on winning my peach.

I am lingering
on the point of frustration
while practicing the
spiritual jujitsu of
a tricky relaxation.

I love the sound that a temple bell makes
It strikes the air with reverberations
It is an invitation to awake
It serves to quiet anticipations
The bell has a tone of solemnity
Which for me is also deeply joyful
It has an odd familiarity
Even though I am anxious and doubtful
It says loving peace is available
And I don't have to get what I'm seeking
When something better is obtainable
It points to an overall releasing
There's a hint that I've known such peace before
I already have what I'm looking for.

The temple bell speaks
of an underlying and
invigorating
simplicity of joyful
being just beyond yearning.

I'm living beyond the temple's borders
And all caught up with winning and losing
I'm worried about what's around the corner
And hungering for objects of my choosing
I'm dangling by a string of my desires
And the wind is making a toy of me
I'm swaying back and forth over a fire
And feeling how my thoughts are scorching me
All I have to do is simply relax
And release what I think that I must get
It is such an insanely simple act
Part of me doesn't want to do it yet
I am a fool living a comedy
Playing a part in greater harmony.

Laughing at myself
I guess is part of the game
rules as long as I'm
not taking my dilemmas
so very seriously.

Messages of peace are all around me
I love listening to wind in the leaves
It is a gentle sound of harmony
I am hearing it tumble sigh and heave
It is a sermon given wordlessly
It's really OK if I have to grieve
And to feel my emotions heartily
As they are signals for me to receive
The *dharma* functions mysteriously
I feel it when I'm listening to trees
Releasing is a possibility
I can free myself and live at my ease
All this striving is an absurdity
It is not helping and can only tease.

Relaxing is the
hardest trick for me pull
off and I do it
when I'm not even thinking
about the need to relax.

I get a sense that I shouldn't hold on
And that I shouldn't be yearning for her
There's a possibility that she's gone
And I can't get back to the way things were
Any master I've heard of can let go
They don't fight against their circumstances
They imitate the water and they flow
I am trying to accept her absence
Sometimes I wonder what she's doing now
And I have to let my mind think like this
I know these thoughts will dissipate somehow
As I am remembering our last kiss
It's funny how my thoughts are like the wind
And when I fight I summon a whirlwind.

My mind and my heart
will whirl as they do until
exhaustion taking
however long it takes and
I have to let it happen.

Once again you snare me with a surprise
I didn't expect you to call again
I forgot you know how to dramatize
I am reluctant but I can't refrain
Only you would ring me at 5 a.m.
No one else would think of calling me then
I'd say I'm not happy — but yes I am
I'd thought we'd connect but didn't know when
You give me an excuse that I can't believe
You say you're paralyzed by the divorce
And you say that I can give you relief
Because you're taking on your ex's force
Your ex-husband is being malicious
And our conversations are delicious.

I'm getting a hint
that this girl has me wrapped
around her pinky
finger and I'm a fool who
couldn't be happier.

The sky is open to the birds and I
Will see a bird or a pair of birds or a
Flock of birds flying in the sky but what
I don't see is where the birds come from

Or where they go and it's easy to
Fix my attention on the feathery
Creatures and neglect the phenomenon
Of the being of the sky that because the

Sky is what it is it has created
The birds to be what the birds have become
Fashioned into many different forms
Of various colors and habits and

I am getting only a glimpse of what
Is happening inside this special moment.

I don't know where the
birds and the sky came from and
don't know where they are
going beyond knowing that
they are woven together.

It's a paradox that when I sense that
I'm much too tense because something within
My expectations led me into a
Cul-de-sac resulting in frustration

And I have reached a point of frustration
That even though I know that I should it
Has become quite difficult to relax
So that even though I want to relax

I do have such a hard time relaxing
And yet when I don't have expectations
And I'm not thinking about the need to
Relax that is precisely when I am

Relaxed and I didn't have to earn my
Relaxation as it's something that happens.

I suppose I could
earn my relaxation by
not having any
expectations but then it's
really hard to do business.

I see a flock of starlings in a bush
And they are making a racket of chirps
And when I approach they become silent
And when I walk away they resume their

Chirping which intrigues me so that again
I approach and again they get quiet
So now I linger to see what they will
Do and after a while now and then and

One at a time they chirp at me with a
Tone I imagine of irritation
And a desire I guess that I would
Go away and leave them to their vital

Communication which to me sounds like
Obsessive and nonsensical gossip.

Perhaps the flock is
the reincarnated soul
of a gossip who
just can't stop talking and so
is now suitably punished.

At the farthest end of my bicycle
Circuit when I am climbing the final
Slope to the utmost elevation of my
Ride I have come to be on the lookout

For a certain red-wing blackbird whom I
Often see perching on one of many
Baby cottonwoods by the side of the
Road and I look forward to seeing the

Bird and hearing it chirp and fly away
As it habitually does but now
I notice sadly all the cottonwoods
After having reached a height of two feet

Have been cut down by the county mower
And going by I don't see the blackbird.

After turning for
the return trip passing
again the missing
cottonwoods I hear and see
the blackbird perched on a post.

On a Saturday afternoon at a
Gathering of my friends at a cabin
On Big Marine Lake we sit watching
A family of loons who are raising

A ruckus and aggressively paddling
Towards a kayaker who got too close
To them and so the kayaker turns and
Is leaving and yet the loons keep chasing

And we watch the drama unfold and a
Couple remarks that the loons also get
Quite agitated in the presence of
Eagles and I do not suppose that the

Eagles are quite as accommodating
As this conscientious kayaker is.

Boundaries are crossed
all the time and decisions
are made about how
aggressively to respond
depending so much on pluck.

Summer is the occasion when I can
Indulge in pleasures otherwise out of
Reach and I look forward to going to
Aldi's once a week and choosing a cart

That perhaps may have a gimpy wheel and
I speed to the bin I'm interested
In not far from the chocolate I can get
In any season so that I can gaze

At the objects of my desire in a
Large bin in the produce department and
I rap them with my knuckles and I've been
Told that it helps in choosing to look for

Yellow patches as an indicator
Of sweetness for the best watermelons.

It's a pivotal
moment when cutting into
the watermelon
and taking the first bite to
appreciate its richness.

If I were a thing of inoffensive
Temperament and not equipped with the
Teeth and prongs of predatory intent
And if all I wanted to do was to

Eat my leaves in peace as the leaves are there
In plentitude to be nibbled wouldn't
It be propitious to blend into
The anonymity and complexity

Of the woody background and I would adopt
A hesitating and a stealthy gait
And on occasion even imitate
The motion of a twig blowing in a

Breeze to avoid the imminent danger
Of exposure seizure and grisly death.

Looking like a twig
amid a billion other
woody doodads the
walking stick merges into
apprehensive quietude.

I fall into a rhythm of the mind
If I wake simmering with energy
At 3 a.m. and too alert to sleep
And the rhythm may be epitomized

As the weight of the past and the future
Which is nothing more than a phantom of
Unpleasant possibilities looming
In the darkness forming into a run

Of what-about-isms which is a way
Of peeking around the corners of what
I think happened or of what might happen
Even though in either case I know that

There's nothing to do at the moment and
It would be better if I could relax.

The propensity
of this rhythm of thought is
dissipation but
its energy dissolves and
I'm OK in the morning.

Rhythms of mind can be likened to a
Hound dog who has a funny habit of
Circling about several times before
It settles down to sleep and just when it's

On the ground and has the appearance of
Being down for the evening it will rise
And resume its circling again and it
Settles and rises and circles again

Over and over and it does no good
For an exasperated observer
To exert force or to distract the dog
With tricks as it's clear that the only thing

To do is let exhaustion do the job
To be followed by rejuvenation.

I guess you could say
that I'm trudging on the road
to liberation
and exhausting myself with
bouts of exaggeration.

The blazing
sun beats on
my leaning
torso — I
pedal my
bike like a
animal.

—*Tekkan*

Everyday Mind XXIII

Humidity
and heat make my
skin sticky with
sweat — the sun is
orange.

The Buddha is said to have remembered
All of his past lives including when he
Was a dolphin which must have reappeared
To him perhaps as one of his happy
Incarnations while I can't see beyond
The boundaries of this apprehensive
Human being which to me is a bond
That is sometimes hard involving pensive
Episodes and I am imagining
What life would be like if I were a stag
Living under the sun and moon roaming
Amid the woods and fields without a lag
Between my sensations and perceptions
With much less complicated decisions.

I am sure there would
be competition with the
other stags over
does but there would also be
much frolic in my swiftness.

The humidity is evident as
Soon as I rise from bed and the air
Is cool early in the morning and has
A tangible liquid quality compared
To what it is in the depth of winter
When I am compelled to use lip balm to
Keep my lips from cracking and it's better
To spread lotion on my skin as I do
To prevent my skin from itching so I
Really do love summer when I may lounge
About the house with all the windows wide
Open without the hinderance to scrounge
For a few moments of natural warmth
Which is a benefit of summer's worth.

By about the mid-
point of afternoon the heat
will begin to sear
the moisture in the air and
everything begins to cook.

Day after day the sun in the summer
Often appears by itself in the sky
And its corona is a bright glimmer
Of white-hot heat which makes everything dry
Despite the humidity — if there are
Many days without the refreshment of
Rain then the yards of grass do become charred
Which is a part of summer I don't love
And last night the sky was cracking with peals
Of thunder and flashing with lightning bolts
Which made the phenomenal sky surreal
Dimming and lighting with electric volts
But today there's no evidence about
Of any rain and we are in a drought.

A couple of days
ago the sunset was a
brilliant orange as
a result of the wildfires
combusting in Canada

Because I am a sincere person who
Usually does do the right thing and
I may slip into self-righteousness too
I do make a lot of mistakes offhand
And later on I think about what I
Did and I'm excessively critical
Of myself thinking I am a bad guy
Not wanting to be hypocritical
Then I'm looking in a funhouse mirror
And all my features and behaviors are
Distorted and my self-image shimmers
Which is a state that is very bizarre
And then I know there's something I should do —
I had better relax — or I am blue.

It's much easier
to do what I gotta do
while forgetting my
self-image which is not
something that's easy to do.

I share my house with a liberated
Being whom I have named Kitcat and he
On occasion can be frustrated
But he is happy ordinarily
His motivations aren't calculated
He thinks and acts instantaneously
Some of the time he is animated
For the bulk of the day he is sleepy
He certainly can be agitated
But I never doubt his sincerity
He's not in the least bit fabricated
He flows with a blissful simplicity
I don't think he's ever been dejected
He's much more likely to be elated.

For some reason he
will suddenly scamper
through the house as fast
as he can without ever
asking for permission first.

I have an uneasy relationship
With the system governing the nation
As our rulers do resort to their whips
To compel behavior to their notions
Which revolve around dividing people
Into perpetrators and rescuers
And victims using a trick that appeals
To our self-pity which is quite sincere
And the trick works because of the use of
Malefactors who need to be defeated
Which rescuers do because of their love
And the agitation is repeated
Ceaselessly because it is so easy
To play the victim and to be lazy.

What would people do
if they realized
they are playing each
of the roles in turn?

Perhaps it's obvious that any way
Of governing a mass of people will
Involve tricks and coercion to convey
Some peace hopefully without overkill
But this is a human predicament
To which I'd rather not devote too much
Thought as I don't want to become hellbent
On winning the argument inasmuch
As squabbling and suffering doesn't
Ever end and I'd rather find my peace
In sincere companionship that isn't
Based on leverage but that brings release
In the awareness and acceptance of
My craziness — as I'm looking for love.

I do need friends who
can occasionally put
disagreements out
of mind as opinions are
needlessly combustible.

She is my maybe lover who wants to
Talk to me on the phone every morning
At 5 a.m. which I've fallen into
Because I think that I may be getting
Somewhere with her but I'm not at all sure
Because at times she will disappear and
And then I am crestfallen and unsure
That we'll ever talk again and I'm stunned
When she comes back into my life again
With a flimsy excuse usually
Having to do with her divorce that strains
Credulity but she talks beautifully
And she has a way of hooking me that
Works — I don't know what to do about that.

I've convinced
myself our talking at
odd hours is harmless
and inconsequential.

I am not without my defenses as
I'm relying on my meditation
And deploying nonchalance with the jazz
Engaging in bantering flirtation
And if you could see me lying in bed
As I am speaking to her you would see
A guy in his element spouting threads
Of ebullient curiosity
Dissecting the absurdities of our
Society and yes I am talking to
Her deep in conversation for an hour
But I could speak to anyone and do
The same as I am a guy who is free
And as casual as I want to be.

And yet she could go away
And I wouldn't get my way
And that would be bad
And I would be sad
But really what can I say?

As I ride my bicycle down a length
Of mostly unused asphalt road every
Afternoon pedaling in the wavelength
Of the summer sun which can be hazy
I can see dozens of grasshoppers on
The road and they are startled by my bike
And they are a surprise to come upon
As everyone will jump and some will strike
Me as I'm passing by and they don't hurt
And I find the phenomenon funny
Which I can't do anything to avert
In summer on asphalt when it's sunny
As this is the season for grasshoppers
In autumn — woolly bear caterpillars

In autumn woolly
bear caterpillars on the
asphalt undulate
across and along my way
but they don't see me at all.

Summer is the time for being lazy
So this poem won't be important and
I can't focus when the air is hazy
So I might as well be sleepy and bland
And write about nothing which is not as
Easy as it might seem as I do need
To be sufficiently careful whereas
If I weren't no one would bother to read
These words and that would be a blow to my
Ego and so today I will confess to you
That for years I've been intending to buy
A hummingbird feeder which I would do
For entertainment but I am lazy
Especially when the air is hazy.

It's so simple to
put up a feeder to see
the hummingbirds but
I haven't got around to
doing it as of today.

As I'm lying awake in bed idly
Waiting for 5 a.m. I can listen
Half-heartedly lackadaisically
To the distant hum of the traffic when
I discover the birds have stopped singing
As they did in spring and I guess they are
Done with mating and summer is bringing
An absence I haven't noticed before
So I keep myself occupied looking
At the clock and listening to the sounds
Of people moving about and driving
Wherever they are going around town
And doing whatever it is they do
Generating an echo as they go.

I'm just waiting for
the clock to get to
5 a.m. when I'll call
and hear her say my name
again and then we'll converse.

I am not as captivated as I
Was and I am practicing nonchalance
With a better estimation of why
We are talking so much in response
To an emptiness and seeing what can
Be done with words at an odd hour of
The day which is perhaps better now than
Not talking in imitation of love
With lighthearted exploration minus
Any expectations of entangled
Consequences as our chat is about
Cavorting with innovative angles
Making a festival of all of our doubts
So we are playing with patterns of words
And being serious would be absurd.

However much we
affect each other I am
able to attend
to my livelihood without
bewildering illusions.

When rushing on the highway it's common
To see the fields of corn or soybeans in
August but today I saw the awesome
Sight of a field of sunflowers wherein
A multitude of yellow faces piqued
My interest with their curious stance
Blossoming at the peak of summer heat
Which I appreciated in a glance
As a blandishment of summer with a
Blazing sun hanging in the sky keeping
Steady pace with my speeding car with the
Army of yellow faces emerging
And vanishing while bringing a smile to
My face which is a lovely thing to do.

Without a word the
sunflowers in serried ranks
gaze patiently up
at the exuberance of
the vibrant summer sunshine.

Please indulge me as I engage my wit
Gathering a ridiculous group of
Words which may in fact entirely fit
Wherein each line follows the one above
Weaving with a semblance of logic which
Gives the impression of progress to a
Satisfying conclusion with a pitch
Inciting curiosity in the
Meaning of words and the significance
Of the ceaseless parading of events
Which is important that it does make sense
Otherwise it wouldn't be worth a cent
As there is a worthiness in spinning puns
Anticipating the punchline is fun.

Can there be sincerity
Coupled with veracity
Pulling you along
With a little song
Leading to serenity?

I need to find a posture that helps to
Keep me balanced and happy even when
I lose a friend and don't know what to do
Because I know the value of a friend
So with an end of communication
Without a reason I can understand
I do feel a familiar frustration
In a feeling of isolation and
I don't believe it's helpful to evade
A sense of loss or to engage in a
Fit of anger or to become afraid
That somehow I am unworthy of the
Solicitude of a friend and so then
I can boomerang and begin again.

I don't believe that
I'm the only one who has
accumulating
grief that disguises itself
under other emotions.

This is the tipping point of the year when
The air in the morning is cool and comes
In through my open windows and yet then
The afternoons are sweltering on some
Days and the heat is beastly which isn't
A condition a person enjoys but
Unconsciously adapts to and doesn't
Notice or bellyache about but what
Does get to me is when I drive about
Town and I can see in scattered patches
The first touches of autumn leaves without
A doubt and every year the sight catches
Me because it points in the direction
Of February and disaffection.

I suffer from a
syndrome called
post-traumatic
February disorder
and can't be talked
out of it.

I am trudging on the road to happy
Destiny putting my faith in a net
Of ancient ideas that I believe
And without knowing what I'm doing yet
I am following the resonance of
My heart which says that each of us is an
Imperishable imbecile of love
Beyond knowing how the journey began
And hemmed about with a forgetfulness
Doing my wholehearted best on this day
And flirting with liberation I guess
But when it is coming I cannot say
Recalling a message that it's easy
Like relaxing within a peaceful breeze.

The way is easy
as long as I do my best
and not worry at
all about the outcome of
everything that I may do.

She likes to go to garage sales and I
Went along with her in the afternoon
And we explored the rolling countryside
As I wanted the chance to be in tune
With her with the casual passage of
Time within the close confines of a car
Even though I really don't share her love
For buying things — we did find a bazaar
Where I bought a pair of cowboy boots and
I don't remember what she got as I
Just wanted to be with her somewhat stunned
When she suddenly wanted to drive by
All the bars where her ex-husband drinks to
See if he was inside and drinking too.

She had me driving
to places I had never
been to and wouldn't
ever return to as I
explored her quirky habits.

Her not being able to let go of
Where her ex-husband is or what he may
Be doing is a signal to me of
A crazy fixation as much to say
That she's obsessed with him and can't let go
Which means that she's thinking more about him
Than me which I've suspected even though
She is with me now the chances are slim
That I'll be the guy she's dreaming about
Especially while she's consumed with her
Failed marriage even though he's a lout
So I'm beginning to think she prefers
Abuse mixed in with excitement perhaps
Which I think clearly leads to a collapse.

Presently she is
like a loaf of half-baked bread
and the yeast has to
be left alone to do its work
before there can be flavor.

What am I going to do now that I can
See that I am not the center of her
Attention and I need to have a plan
That's sensibly based on what I prefer
Because I like her company and as
I am engaged in a fantasy of
Possessing her — so should I quit? Whereas
I love the feeling of being in love
And maybe we can keep talking without
Doing any harm to each other or
Mostly to me if I can figure out
How to hang in there and open the door
To the possibility of love — or
To keep her from becoming a big chore?

There is curiosity
Inside our verbosity
Involving some clues
Of what we could do
With some reciprocity.

This is a quiet thunder rumbling from
A distance and it has soft edges and
A gentle touch not like a booming drum
And not like the sudden claps and cracks and
The tearing of the sky that I have heard
But instead it is so grand and wondrous
Which is difficult to put into words
When definitions are superfluous
And this thunder does mean something to me
As it reveals an echoing vastness
Of horizons I'm not able to see
Of mysteries concealed by the darkness —
This thunder is casting a soothing spell
It is a summons like a temple bell.

Also the patter
of continuing rain has
a gentle cadence
coming through open windows
carried along in a breeze.

My experience now is to watch the
Ups and downs of my daily life and to
Know when I'm not at my best and that a
New circumstance is arriving to do
Whatever it will to change my mood and
I realize that I can't wrench myself
Into a better mood but that I can
Learn to surf emotions as life itself
Is a continuing vibration of
Ups and downs much like the crests and the troughs
Of waves and I will weather my share of
Disappointment and success and slough off
The weight of serious expectations
And learn to live with my fluctuations.

It's easy to talk
this way but there's a trick in
really living this
way which involves letting go
of serious assumptions.

This habit I have of writing sonnets
Is kind of crazy and doesn't make sense
As I can't see that I'll ever profit
Financially and I have no pretense
Of doing more than just playing with words
Putting them together in odd ways and
Deploying irony may be absurd
Upsetting expectations if I can
By relying on my sincerity
Traipsing in a definite direction
Practicing my verbal dexterity
Not caring about remuneration
Because — as much as you — I want to see
What this crazy poem is going to be.

Don't ask me how this
poem is going to finish
because I haven't
a clue until I blunder
on a happy finale.

The birds are not as noisy as they were
During their springtime exuberance as
The mating season is done and they are
Liberated now and have much less sass
About defending their territory
But they can be heard now and again as
In sporadic joyful oratory
And they do lighten my heart as I pass
Setting me free from the clutch of my thoughts
And the birds are often invisible
Hidden in foliage but I can spot
Them in the air when I'm able
To absorb myself in my surroundings
And attending to birds is a wingding.

Foliage hides
the absolutely
unique twisting
of each branch.

I'm not liberated because I'm still
Engaged in pursuit of this woman who
Knows very well that I'm obsessed and will
Call her every morning and join her too
At least once a week for lunch or supper
In restaurants or cafés and a day
Ago I drove her to a carpet store
As I'm doing my best to find a way
To insinuate my presence into
Her life and it's all very well for the
Buddha to be autonomous and to
Not be concerned about results in a
Meditative state of serenity
But I do want her reciprocity.

She says she talks to
me more than to anyone
else in her life and
that's the sort of comment that
keeps me so interested.

The other day she recruited me with
Several other big guys to move her
Oak armoire which was such a heavy lift
Out of her ex's house and up the stairs
To her townhouse and I was the guy on
The left front of it and to pull it up
To strain my back and legs to come upon
One more step above without giving up
And in between each heave its weight would drop
With a prodigious thud and it almost
Smashed my foot but we made it to the top
After I had expended my utmost
Energy and I am glad that it is done
Because there are other ways to have fun.

The ordeal was
another way for me to
ingratiate my
potency into her good
graces — at least I hope so.

It's a question when I'm assembling
Words whether I'm giving preference to
My ears or eyes as I will be saying
Words over again and listening to
The way they tickle my ears and also
I will be counting syllables to put
A pleasing number within each line so
I can measure every metrical foot
And I will be taking the time to rhyme
Coming at the end of every line but
It is not my habit at every time
To be obvious and so to see what
I am doing you have to read the words
To discover whether they are absurd.

If there isn't a
sufficiently pleasing thread
of meaning to keep
you following me you would
stop listening or reading.

I've got to carry on with this girl and
Not give a damn whether what I want comes
About or not as I do what I can
And am learning at least a little some
Of the ploys involved in being relaxed
And passionate at the same time and how
I can do that and not become attached
To the results is a trick that somehow
Comes along perhaps only through doing
Exactly what I'm doing and it might
Be more propitious to be taking
More time to see whether she is the right
One for me as there are indications
That she likes to perpetrate frustrations.

Being together
doesn't necessarily
mean that we are
getting somewhere or
will arrive together.

I'm ashamed to be laughing at people
By looking at a website that shows their
Hideous tattoos like the fellow who
Emblazoned the words "No Regerts" on his

Arm as a determined declaration
Of stupidity or the guy who sports
A frightening black widow spider that
Covers a quarter of his face or the

Sad and monstrous depictions due to
The incompetence of the artist of
A parent's daughter or son as I can
Imagine the weight of embarrassment

And horror and regret on the morning
Afterward that surely must come to them.

Scrolling through dozens
of photos of hideous
tattoos inspires
fascination similar
to a traffic accident.

Kitcat manages to express himself
Very well without the benefit of
Words as he employs a variation
Of yowls with the tenor of a rising

Or a descending quality and he
May on occasion be monotone but
He is sure to moderate the length of
His utterance and there's a difference

Of emphasis along a spectrum from
Quiescence to mildly interested
To insistence to excited and to
Absolute vehemence as when I tread

On his tail that elicits from me my
Most abashed and heartfelt apology.

When he wants a treat
he knocks the container off
of the counter and
expresses a simple yowl that
cannot be misunderstood.

Ours is a culture of videos and
Press releases and of the branding and
The endorsement of celebrity
Products and of accepted opinions

Perpetuating associations
Of inclusion or exclusion and our
Hearts are burdened with the task of
Finding where and with whom we will find home

Amid the susceptibility of
Human fallibility and I would
Like to transform resentments into
The acknowledgment of hurts whereby

I no longer need to blame anyone
Which to me would be a liberation.

I would like to be
as light as a feather with
as many people
as possible while choosing
my skirmishes carefully.

What I take from the Bhagavad Gita
Is the direction to be wholehearted
While letting go of results which is a
Trick when I'm in a pattern of waking

In the night with energized thoughts that are
Heavy with misapprehensions about
The people I know whom I'm not getting
Along with as well as I would like to

Arousing me from my bed to fold my
Legs and meditate in the darkness to
See what may be accomplished with a
Posture of tension counterbalanced with

A relaxation of consciousness that
Allows for the relinquishing of thoughts.

The tension of the
spine and the relaxation
of the shoulders make
for the combustion of an
energy that burns my thoughts.

I was pedaling in ignorance up
The hills and along the long stretches of
The countryside and comparing myself
To the reported average speed of

The riders of the *Tour de France* mindful
Of what a laggard I would appear next
To they who have transformed the muscles of
Their bodies into a sleek resemblance

Of the tubular composition of
Their bicycles apart from their hefty
Thighs and calves that pump incessantly with
Enviable speed leaving me behind

While I was ignorantly working so
Much harder than was necessary.

I had only to
pump air into the tires
to reach the proper
pounds per square inch and then I
could race like a maniac

Whether I should gamble and go to my
45th high school reunion was the
Question at the bowling alley and bar
Because at the 40th I learned that

Most of the group were strangers to me and
Our talking was an awkward groping for
Connections that couldn't be founded on
The past because I couldn't recall it

But on the other hand I've traveled to
Several nations and I have stories
To tell and I could start a new friendship
And I haven't been pummeled nearly as

Much with the ugly stick as the others
Have and I could have a romantic fling.

At the 40th
an enthusiastic and
inebriated
fellow bellowed my name but
who he was I couldn't say.

I found a white feather on the grass by
The river and the shaft is thick at its
Base and narrows as it goes along and
Is pointedly thin at the feather's end

And the shaft is weightlessly hollow — while
The vane of the feather is translucent
And on one side the vane is narrow and
Has a straight edge but on the other it's

Wide and curves in a graceful line — and when
I swish the feather up and down beside
My cheek as if it were a Japanese
Fan I can feel a wafting of the air

And maybe the feather came from a gull
Or it might have been left by a pigeon.

From now on I will
wear the feather inside the
band of my straw hat
as an epitome of
a natural jewelry.

I keep a marble urn on top of a
Chest of drawers in my bedroom and in the
Urn there are a dozen peacock feathers and
And the urn itself is sandy colored

And speckled with pink and red rosettes and
The peacock feathers are explosions of
Frilly extravagance and these things have
Been inside my room for decades and I

Don't think about them very much but
When I do I see the manmade shape of the
The urn that shows the hidden beauty of
The earth and I notice the feathers that

Are bright exotica of a bird that
Also has an origin like the earth.

The feathers and the
urn are like bookends
of phenomena that
arose from emptiness.

The ancient Bhagavad Gita concerns
Itself with subtleties of nature and
Of consciousness consoling me with a
Pronouncement beyond my understanding

Saying that consciousness continues through
Lifetimes bordered by a forgetfulness
That prevents me from becoming weary
And disheartened with poignant memories

So that the imperishable game of
Life is fresh in the moment and I may
Act spontaneously without worry
Of losing my chances forever as

I am free to experience loss and
Suffer and triumph again and again.

The thing to do is to
act wholeheartedly
without worry
about results.

I enjoyed my high school reunion
Last night a little ashamed that classmates
Remembered me much better than I did
With them but the more we talked the more I

Recognized and the evening presented
A sweet poignancy in the person of
Heidi Junker who rode on the school bus
With me on whom I had a crush but I

Was too shy to summon my impulses
To fruition and Heidi was surprised
And amused by my confession saying
She would have dated me as she sadly

Thought that because her dad was the quirky
Mayor she lost many chances for dates.

I remember her
as bespeckled and cute with
such pleasing curves
that inspired sensuous
and curious impulses.

Jim Morton found me again on Facebook
And we shared our memories on the phone
Of living in Kyoto Japan 30
Years ago and we reminisced about

Teaching English to the Japanese and
About being able to escape and
Go to *Hoshinnji* where the Zen master
Harada would hold practice periods

Of silent meditation in pursuit
Of the *Dharma* in the sincere manner
Of any of the ancient masters from
Hundreds of years ago in China or

Japan because that is how *Dharma*
Is transmitted — from master to student.

Harada filled my
abdomen with a glowing
warmth during our last
private interview showing
me true generosity.

I met Jim through a teaching buddy and
I drove a scooter to his home after
My evening lessons and we would sit in
Meditation and lift heavy barbells

And he introduced me to *Hoshinnji*
And he became my bridge to the *Dharma*
And he opened a door to a quest for
Liberation which I'm still pursuing

And Jim is a big fellow with skillful
Woodworking hands and a cheerful and a
Gentle comportment and a twinkle in
His eyes reflecting a secret which is

Always open to anyone lucky
Enough to have stumbled upon the path.

Jim and I agree
that there are many
American Zen
priests but very few
genuine masters.

There is a world beyond my thoughts where things
Happen spontaneously in every
Direction ceaselessly and I would love
To be in harmony without the weight

Of the burden of my thoughts and I am
Bound with worries and cravings and sometimes
I'm awake hours before the dawn and
I realize that I am clouding the

World with the impetus of my worries
And cravings and I haven't discovered
The way to liberation yet but at
Least I do have a clue about the

Nature of my troubles and having a
Companion like Jim is very helpful.

The *Dharma* is transmitted
from person to person
and a liberated
personality is
key.

Jim is still doing all of the things he
Used to do three decades ago such as
Japanese calligraphy and drawing
Kanji with his horsehair brushes with a

Flourish of his wrist and hand and to
Me the letters look like blotches of ink
On paper but to Jim they are forms that
Rise up in three dimensions and he sees

The flowing dance of the brush as if in
Imitation of the graceful verve
Of a *katana* slicing through the air
And there are very few people with the

Discernment to appreciate the pith
Of the motion — but Jim keeps doing it.

Jim's happy to do
repeatedly over the
decades an art that
is unappreciated
because he's still improving.

Jim's gentle and baritone words brought back
To me the memories that I could have
Gained in no other way as I relish
Being a companion on Jim's journey

Gleaning through his eyes the ambience of
The San Francisco Zen Center and his
Acquaintance with its founding Zen master
Shunryu Suzuki who upended his

Students by breaking cherished traditions
In one case tricking an earnest novice
Into eating a hamburger using
Humor and intelligence to make an

Unforgettable point driving home a
Ploy of spontaneous innovation.

Using traditions by
upsetting the traditions
effectively and
humorously is a ploy
of a liberated guy.

Kitcat is perilous like a tiger
He doesn't care that he's only pint size
Extending no more than a foot lengthwise
I know him to be a ready biter
With the inclination of a fighter
He stares ferociously with tiger's eyes
With an intensity to hypnotize
Taut and tense in every nervy fiber
While he knows my habits — and I know his
I sing him tunes of nonsense quality
He flops on the floor and shows his belly
Does he want to play? He certainly does
He's quite capable of frivolity
And I know his belly feels like jelly.

He has the ferocity
Along with sinuosity
Pouncing with pleasure
He's very clever
But he lacks verbosity.

I've not been one to follow conventions
Instead I've taken odd romantic jobs
Shorn of the dignity preferred by snobs
I know I cherish certain pretensions
That come with a load of expectations
One can't seek clarity and be a slob
Or cater to the whims of vicious mobs
I want to be clear in my intentions
And to play with words and make a living
Forgoing a rewarding salary
To linger with the inexpressible
To play with notions of awakening
Though my method may be a fallacy
I do aim to be comprehensible.

It may not be credible
Or even respectable
To try to profit
By writing sonnets
But it is delectable.

I do understand your emotions and
Know that you're having a difficult time
And seeking for balance in the meantime
Letting go of a marriage that has spanned
Maybe three decades and that you can't stand
Being dispensed with when you're in your prime
Which indicates a ton of loss and I'm
Not disoriented and am on hand
To divert the agitation of your
Thoughts with the exploration of my words
As there's no need to be stuck in the past
When you could be hopeful and open doors
And as I am you could be looking toward
A liberation and a peace that lasts.

Driving around to
bars to see whether his car
is parked outside
isn't fun and I'd rather
do anything else with you.

I get a boost talking to you every
Morning on the phone when most people are
Still sleeping in bed and it is bizarre
That we can be exchanging repartee
Consuming an hour in reverie
So who would care to get drunk in a bar
Or to be constantly picking at scars
And be writhing about in dependency
When intimacy alleviates so
Much of our compulsive agitation
And there's no substitute for feeling loved
Which I missed through years of living solo
And now that's ending with conversation
As you're making me feel understood.

Some days I wake up
early and count the minutes
until I can call
and hear again your cheerful
voice I am accustomed to.

The American soldier is so poorly
Appreciated by Americans
Who don't care much about Afghanistan
While soldiers take honor seriously
And they dedicate their lives to duty
As they follow orders and garrison
The most belligerent and distant land
Not questioning the nation's policy
But America suffers poor leadership
So blame the presidents and generals
And our governing class is terrible
Lost in petty venal partisanship
Where the blame-shifting is perennial
And their constant lies are contemptible.

The burden of our
nation's mistakes falls upon
honor-bound soldiers
and their families while the
elites appropriate wealth.

Arrogance and incompetence are on
The rise in American leadership
Coming with deceiving partisanship
In a news media that strings along
Narratives designed not only to con
Americans but also to equip
Politicians with propaganda stripped
Of heartfelt regard for the truth forgone
Because our intellectuals are more
Interested in power and control
And now Americans are bitterly
Divided which is harder to ignore
As every calamity takes a toll
And politicians fail repeatedly.

Righteous
propaganda
inspires
fellow-feeling in
everyone except
its targets.

I am a droplet of the universe
And I embody its propensities
For dissolution and ascendency
And I do determine the impetus
Of direction from the secret impulse
Of my thoughts that pivot incessantly
In a delicate dance tentatively
Balanced between the better and the worse
And I need to be aware when the tenor
Of my thinking is mostly negative
And I'm soliciting unhappiness
And then it helps very much to explore
The releasing of thoughts generative
Of a welcome relaxation and peace.

Circumstances do
impose leverage over
times but a watchful
and persisting gentleness
emboldens optimism.

I traveled to Ohio to visit
Relatives and to take my elderly
Mother to meet her sister tenderly
Reuniting the two from the limits
Of distance and time making explicit
All the buried memories heartily
At a surprise party sprung cheerfully
On my mother's sister and we did it
To celebrate her sister's 90th
Birthday and the sisters will have very
Much to talk and to reminisce over
And the moment of meeting took my breath
Watching their reunion became teary
With a wealth of liveliness left over.

Beloved husbands
children
grandchildren
great-grandchildren
the vanishing world —
so much to discuss.

The fingers and ankles and the balls of
The feet are vital components of a
Bicycle rider as I learned with the
Use of a light carbon fiber bike of
Superior quality with the shoes of
A different clip-on style and with the
Gear shifting mechanism needing a
Challenging and puzzling sequence of
Finger manipulation new to me
Which I had to remember on the fly
And my ankles are attuned to the twist
That frees the shoe from the pedal but I
Couldn't click into the pedal and missed
Much too often as I strove to apply
Directional pressure to get the gist.

My brother loaned me
the use of his best bike which
unexpectedly
demanded a different
display of dexterity.

I am a simple guy with a speedy
Aluminum bicycle at home but
My brother drives to distant trails and puts
His bikes on a rack on a luxury
Car and he can track his proximity
Heart rate and wind speed and I don't know what
Else but besides all that he has the guts
To ride like he's crazy repeatedly
Over the years and I was proud to keep
Up and surprised that I could fixing my
Attention on him because suddenly
He'd race and the rivers and trees would sweep
By but after several good hours I
Did get tired and moved exhaustedly.

Days later he sent
me an email with graphs of
elevation with
exact locations and a
sum of our average speed.

I am reading an Agatha Christie
Murder mystery about what appeared to
Be a double suicide having to
Do with a respectable and happy
Couple of British high society
Which occurred a decade previous to
The events of the story which turned to
An examination of memory
Involving insights gleaned from the British
Empire giving weight to the phrase that
"An elephant remembers" implying
That telling clues however diminished
Lie dormant within incomplete views that
Disparate people hold that need sifting.

Like the elephants
people cherish opinions
precariously
based on uncertain facts that
are disappearing targets.

The furrowed brow and comprehending eyes
Of elephants are curious clues to
A sensibility with a strange view
That implies that they surely could be wise
To predicaments and choices with ties
Of volatility of what to do
Within the circumstances leading to
Their haphazard impulses when surprised
And if the expression is true that the
Elephants remember the insults or
The generosity of people from
Years ago then they are truly due a
Sympathetic respect and a rapport
Earned from the mystery from which we come.

If I were born with
the trunk the enormous girth
the feet and the ears
of an elephant I would
cavort with lumbering strength.

It's better to admit that it's bigger
Than you and over time it will beat you
Down and will thoroughly discourage you
And you've heard enough lies to be bitter
And you do yourself damage to bicker
And after the divorce it's clear you're through
So what is it that you're trying to do?
As you know he's not a normal drinker
And an alcoholic won't get better
And if he's not willing to save himself
You know there is nothing that you can do
You're divorced — it's done — so be a quitter
It's way past time to take care of yourself —
I've reached a limit of what I can do.

You've got to admit
that you've hit a wall with him
there's nothing to do
other than to let him deal
with his alcoholism.

There is a way to get out of trouble
Whether a person is alcoholic
Or is one who loves an alcoholic
And it really is inevitable
And after it's done it's not a puzzle
You've got to admit that the guy is sick
And then surrendering becomes the trick
Then finally things are manageable
There just *has* to be an end to fighting
When every effort to control it flops
The only answer is relaxation
I know even though he might be dying
Your intention to cure it has to stop —
Try to let go of your expectations.

When I finally
admitted that I was an
alcoholic a
weight was lifted from my
shoulders and I became free.

She says — I went over to his house the
Very home where we raised our family
And I saw the mess of his apathy —
The counter was cluttered with dishes — the
Carpet was dirty — things were scattered — the
Dog was tense and ready to bite me —
There was a sense of unreality
With him sitting on the stairs and in a
Daze in his underwear before he had
To dress for work and seeing him like that
I thought he's not attractive anymore
And I couldn't be mad but sure was sad
To see the misery he's arrived at
With our history which I can't ignore.

And now I don't have
to be thinking about him
any more and I
can be free from whatever
compulsive needs I had.

I say that — I try to remember when
I'm sad or unhappy for whatever
Reason or when I'm feeling the pressure
Of being separate from people in
My life that the Eastern *Dharma* begins
With suffering and that I will suffer
Because of my stubbornness whenever
I can't let go of something but I can
Remember and see the simplicity
Of the point that if I'm not clinging to
What I want then I won't be suffering
But I admit I have difficulty
Doing my best at letting go — and to
Be better at that I am practicing.

Doing my best while
letting go of results is
a propitious
trick of relaxation that
I haven't begun to master.

I can't practice very well on my own
And I need people who share at least some
Of the ideas I'm using who can come
To understanding me and to be shown
How better it is than being alone
And I think you know where I'm coming from
And I'm telling you that it means a ton
To be listening to you on the phone
As we both know from experience that
Alcoholism is deadly and there's
So much more to be had from life than to
Be isolated and lonely in what
Is certain to become a mess that spares
No misery — not knowing what to do.

If what I say sounds
crazy imagine how things
would be if I had
no one to mitigate the
nonsense inside of my head.

I catch myself at odd moments saying
To myself when nobody but me is
Listening that "she is my girl" and is
This really true as I am suspecting
That my subconsciousness is asserting
That "she is my girl" and in fact she does
Love me and in idle moments she does
Care for me as much as I am caring
About her? But perhaps it's true that by force
Of will I am repeating a guess that
I desperately hope to be the truth
When I know deep down that I can't enforce
My wishes on reality and that
I may be fooling myself with half-truths.

I do have to watch
such messages when part of
me is trying to
convince the other part they're
true — when they may not be true.

There was the nagging incident when I
Waited at a restaurant for 40
Minutes alone for her and she hardly
Expressed a reason and as a nice guy
I didn't quibble wanting to get by
Without unpleasantness — and again we
Were at a restaurant being carefree
Having a good time when things went awry
When she saw a man she knew before and
Invited him to join us unmindful
Of my feelings and the two of them were
Eagerly engaged excluding me and
I do admit that I was resentful
Lonely frustrated and doubtful of her.

Another time she
spoke to a waiter about
me in a manner
that wasn't quite respectful
as I sat by stoically.

When we meet together in public there
Is a good chance that we'll have fun and that
I'll drive home satisfied and thinking that
The night couldn't have gone better aware
Of emotional burdens that she bears
But sometimes it's true that I'm feeling flat
With worries that I don't want to look at
With nagging suspicions it may be fair
To question her regard for me and yet
When we speak on the phone before the dawn
Every day I am able to express
My heartfelt words and then I do forget
My doubts because of the joy I live on
Because conversation feels like success.

The facility
of expression that we share
in morning hours
has in it for me the joy
of being comprehended.

A spasm of the neck afflicted her
When she was alone in her living room
Which was a sharp searing pain I assume
While I was on my bike and nowhere near
And perhaps it felt like a sudden tear
And afterwards there was persisting gloom
Which she felt in the emergency room
As being old isn't easy for her
And so I was called to the hospital
I noticed she was well attended to
But my mother was weary and confused
She isn't moving well and she's brittle
So we have a course of treatment to do
And another stage of life is opened.

There were episodes
in the past with spasms in
her back that she's been
able to overcome so
there's reason to be hopeful.

I've noticed it and perhaps you have too
That dust accumulates inside a house
It would be helpful to have a loving spouse
There is so much maintenance to do
With little nagging chores to get through
And I have no remedy to espouse
No easy revelation to announce
There are some adjustments to attend to
When one of a married couple dies first
There was the joy of many loving years
Looked back upon with appreciation
Then suddenly that time of life is burst
And we are presented with strange new cares
Can we make a reevaluation?

My mom was always
the quiet underlying
security of our
family cooking suppers
and civilizing her kids.

I had an idea — but forgot it
I had it — but I'm not remembering
Now I'm stuck and sitting here questioning
Sometimes I suspect I'm losing my wits
Perhaps by now I'm only a half-wit
I was in the habit of note-taking
Reading a note is reawakening
But I've been lazy and not doing it —
You see it's so important to be on
The lookout for the spark of insight that
Springs a poem and when it comes I need to
Recognize it appreciate it on
The spot and seize on the catalyst that
Makes possible all the hullabaloo.

It's like entering
a room and realizing
you have forgotten
why you came — inspiration
slips quickly through my fingers.

Agatha Christie is an expert at
Revealing a person's character with
A quirk of speech in her dialogues with
A spice of intriguing happenings that
Impels me to keep reading even at
A time of night when I'd be sleeping with
My dreams as she is a maestro wordsmith
Who makes me jealous dangling her clues that
May amount to nothing or not but there
Are too many clues mixed with the details
Of plot to keep track of and I truly
Love her depiction of the British where
Subtle class distinctions make for blackmail
Within the rank of high society.

She reveals the
weakness and the meanness in
the disorder of
human nature directing
motivation to murder.

Agatha Christie clued me into the
Fact that I am a "dipsomaniac"
Which is a word meaning alcoholic
Which says I'm a "dipso" added to a
"Mania" which means I could be a
"Maniac" which is quite a verbal whack
Which implies people like me need smacks
To keep us soberly sensible in a
 World that expects much better of us
And I'm not going to quibble about that
As we have maniacal qualities
But I am not a dilophosaurus
Which was a toothy dinosaur that
Had much worse antisocial qualities.

Agatha Christie
uses her verbosity
quite responsibly
and she only had to use
the word once to make her point.

My house which I have almost finished paying
For is looking a little worse for wear and
The joints between my pipes are leaky and
I've put up with it for a while thinking
That my iron pipes will be expanding
Because colder weather is coming and
Isn't that what iron does when cold and
I saw how stupid I was admitting
I had to call a plumber reluctantly
Because I'm stingy but I did make the call
For a plumber and he said that pipes will
Leak and then he got to work and quickly
Discovered that a rubber hose had caused all
The mess which he fixed and gave me a bill.

I am a wordy
intellectual who could
convince himself that
iron pipes will expand in
cold and therefore stop the leaks.

I received an email today about
The Sistine Chapel which included a
Virtual tour which presented me a
Panoramic view and I could check out
The exquisite designs and expand out
The smallest details with a flick of the
Wrist and with a shift of the mouse of a
Mac computer which is nothing to pout
About and the email informed me that
Pope Julius became impatient with
Michelangelo because he believed
The artist was too dilatory at
The job and so the Pope questioned him with
Pique: Why was he so slow at what he did?

Michelangelo
answered Pope Julius
by saying that he
was still learning —
"Ancora Imparo."

Now we have entered into September
Which does make me somewhat melancholy
I'm a little sad — but not unhappy
As I'm at an age when I remember
All the many times we've turned this corner
Maybe I am prematurely sappy
A little somber — though not unhappy
This isn't the darkness of December
There will be plenty of warm days to come
I'll ride my bike as often as I can
And savor every change of the season
By watching the quality of the sun
And noticing its diminishing span
As summer is reaching its completion.

The glare of the sun
is diminishing in the
evening and the light
touching my cottonwood leaves
has a golden glow about it.

In the affairs of state involving the
Conduct of warfare and of strategy
It's painful to perceive complacency
And negligence in the betters of a
Republic who wouldn't when they had the
Time order their plans with competency
So at the point of crisis they betray
Citizens and faithful allies and the
Families of our warriors even
In the event surrendering people
Into the clutches of the enemy
Unto death whatever one believes in
When our leaders lie it's contemptible
To covet power without decency.

Thousands of faithful
allies and American
citizens were left
behind in Afghanistan
by America's betters.

The dwelling where my family lived for
Most of my childhood is on the north hill
Of Stillwater and so the rooms are filled
With memories almost forgotten or
Over the verge of consciousness stored
Latently somehow within me but still
Available being bygone until
A turn of my thinking opens a door
For instance when I notice an object
Among hundreds of other objects that
Returns to present awareness a tang
Of emotional insight that connects
Whomever I was with who I am that
Delivers to me a walloping pang.

The oak rocking chair
In the living room where my Dad
used to watch football
on Sunday afternoons has
comfortable resonance.

My mom suffered a spasm of her neck
And now she can't turn her head to the left
She needs looking after and so I check
Whether she is eating and getting rest
The doctor prescribed her several pills
She needs reminding of when to take them
The pain in her head is making her ill
She's not defeated — just a little glum
But I am noticing that she's forgetful
She can't recall what happened yesterday
She eats so little that I get fretful
When I push her to eat she does give way
To get better she needs some directions
She doesn't have so many objections.

When awake she stays
bent over on the couch with
a hot or cold pack
pressed upon her neck as the
doctor has directed her.

The clouds are drifting to the south today
And the sky is filled with warm gentle light
And there was a hurricane yesterday
But not a hint of that in this sunlight
Much of America was torn by storm
So many houses were struck and destroyed
I do forget that such storms are the norm
And that tragedies are hard to avoid
The leaves today are suffused with the light
The glow of sun is blissfully peaceful
The turn toward autumn is beautifully bright
I have no reason to be regretful
The trouble is over the horizon
In the south it is hurricane season.

I would much rather
suffer the impending cold
and the blizzards of
Minnesota than the news
of another hurricane
brewing off of the Gulf Coast.

I've been noticing the patterns of birds
I saw a flock of sparrows yesterday
How can I capture them only with words?
We heard a boisterous blue jay today
The jay interrupted a Zoom meeting
And we absorbed it on a microphone
Most of my views of birds are fleeting
I see them flying between trees alone
Some days ago I saw a chickadee
On my bicycle I spotted a gull
There are turkey vultures in twos and threes
I don't believe I've heard a vulture's call
So many birds will be migrating soon
They will be returning again in June.

Toucans flamingos
Galápagos penguins and
various parrots
are birds that never venture
to frozen Minnesota.

She's wearing a bright yellow summer dress
With a string top exposing her shoulders
It's apparent she's dressing to impress
Stimulating an urge to embrace her
I'm guessing excitement can be helpful
Prompting me to be alert and fluent
To play with my words — and to be cheerful
I'm even able to experiment
To venture a little pleasing teasing
Hinting at her availability
Expressing that she's very appealing
That she could well be another Sherry
In response she's very animated
This is better than anticipated.

The Kung Pao Chicken
with spicy chili sauce and
with green onions and
with red chili peppers went
by without much noticing.

Sherry is a woman who works with her
Sherry teases guys and gets rid of them
She is not like Sherry but if she were
I'd never be beneath anyone's thumb
I love the conversation and banter
Tonight we shared devoted attention
She didn't make remarks to the waiter
There were no moments of apprehension
She's very savvy and stimulating
And does make me feel appreciated
Sometimes she can be almost insulting
And I don't like being disrespected
I will play along with her for a while
More often than not she's making me smile.

I am thinking how
much easier it would be
not to be thought of
as having to call her and
entertain her so often.

I parked my Corolla along the edge
Of the parking lot lengthwise because the
Places in the middle were taken and
I did have misgivings but I ignored

Them and when the meeting finished and I
Returned to my car I was surprised by
An apologetic young woman who
Confessed to backing into my car and

We examined a slight dent disrupting
The stylish aerodynamic angles
Of my driver's side rear passenger door
And I didn't call the police to make

A report because she waited for me
And I trusted she would do the right thing.

She didn't return
my calls and thus refused to
cooperate with
the insurance claim so the
dent will be decorative.

The sky to the south overlooking the
River valley is full of the morning
Light gentle and warm and let it be a
Replacement of my thoughts as the geese are

Spanning the expanse in an elegant
Line of flight and I don't know where they are
Going and the sprinklers in the park have
Stopped and drops of water are speckling a

A steel park bench and refracting the light
With rainbow brilliance and three crows chase each
Other past the maple tree intent on
Some kind of competition and the oak

Spreads its green leaves unmindful of the change
Of the seasons poised and prospering now.

I listen to my
sober dipsomaniacs
and speak in my turn
but I am also inside
the phantasmagoria.

I used Agatha Christie by reading
Her novel up until the moment I
Went to bed happily yesterday at
The point when the murder was announced and

Every character is smoldering with
Hidden motivations and there's a fog
Of puzzling ambience to chew over
Which fascinates me and allows me to

Forget about myself so that chances
Are I won't wake up at 3 a.m. with
Enough nervous energy to prevent
Me from sleeping and even if I wake

I can dwell on the labors of Hercule
Poirot or on Jane Marple's cleverness.

The mayhem of an
Agatha Christie novel
is preferable
to the moroseness of my
3 a.m. meditations.

I can put the words on this paper that
Contain the meaning of the emptiness
Of things that propose that there is no birth
And no death and also no being and

No nonbeing and that there can be no
Defilement when there is no purity
And that along with the body there is
Emptiness and that the body is not

Different from emptiness but is in
Fact the same as emptiness and there are
No eyes and ears and nose and tongue and skin
No sight and sound and smell and taste and touch

And the meanings of these words imply these
Words are nonsensically meaningless.

Yet for some reason
for thousands of years people
have taken these words
to heart and a few of them
profess realization.

On this particular piece of paper
Bound together with other pages on
The left and surrounded by margins there
Are words arranged into orderly lines

Wherein letters are stuck to each other
That compose syllables which may be read
Silently or spoken out loud and the
Combined meaning flows along from the left

To the right and you may read up or down
Or right to left and obtain gibberish
Or you may follow convention to get
The gist of the meaning and thus achieve

Comprehension and in conclusion you
May decide if the trip was worth taking.

After the trip the
import of the words lingers
for a moment but
eventually they will
dissolve into emptiness.

Seeing school buses going by on the
Streets again after the summer break is
Over brings back memories of concerns
Lasting over decades whether my kids

Were learning measuring up and getting
Along mixing with the others of their
Age as they were already laying down
The patterns of their lives being lonely

Hurt and disappointed along with their
Successes while I questioned if I was
Doing enough and where would the money
To pay for college come from which was a

Hurdle I didn't dwell on much but I
Guessed we'd find a way to graduation.

They are
intelligent
educated
graduated
engaged in life
and out of the house.

I am stubborn and don't want to close the
Windows of my house even though the air
Before dawn when I wake and move about
Is becoming more than cool and verging

Into chilly and I gave up going
Barefoot and acquiesced to wearing socks
Inside slippers and I put on my long
Pants and long sleeves and I am accustomed

Now to the preponderance of darkness
Extending further into the morning
As I fold into the lotus posture
And notice the absence of birdsong and

The percolation of coffee and the
Dog barking at a point in the distance.

I am not ready
yet to give in and to close
the windows and then
to resort to the furnace
and thus to be hunkered down.

The link on the Internet that gives me a
A panoramic and intimate view
Of the Sistine Chapel and lets me see
The twelve high windows through which the light shines

Helped me to picture Michelangelo
On a scaffold standing and reaching up
Awkwardly to the ceiling as he took
The drops of paint that speckled his face for

The four long years of his labor and how
Important those windows must have been to
Let in the daylight illuminating
And clarifying what he had done and

How much further there was to go in the
Creation of his view of Creation.

Michelangelo
lived without the blessing of
electricity
confined within the borders
of vivid darkness and light.

I see it in the air in September
Before the bulk of the leaves begin to
Flower into autumn colors as the
Shadows lengthen in the twilight of the

Morning and evening and the haze that's so
Typical of summer afternoons cleared
And is replaced by a crispness and when
I ride my bicycle the heat is not

Present and the glare of the sun does not
Bleach the color from the trees but instead
The lustrous leaves are tinged with the yellow
Of the sun and there is quiet and it

Is cool and the sun in the open sky
Retains its brilliance but is past its peak.

We had rainy days
and the fields of corn have grown
tall and the grass is
green and growing but there is
a conclusion in the air.

Decisions have to be made as my Mom
Is forgetting whether she took all of
Her pills and she can't remember when to
Take them and I'm not there enough to keep

Track and after her neck spasm her head
Continuously aches and she told my
Sister a different story about
The nature of her accident than she

Told me involving a fall that I was
Unaware of and it's tricky to know
Whether she's eating and drinking enough
To sustain herself and she's sleeping and

I don't want to disturb her yet but I
Do need to get her to the clinic soon.

Relaxed
and poised

is the best
I can do

waiting for
inspiration.

Mom is an accumulator of stuff
And her house is tidy and organized
And every drawer and closet is full
Of things that were put there decades ago

And we children have always known the days will
Come when the sanctuary of comfort
That my mother has woven will have to
Be undone and the weightiness and the grief

Involved with the task is a dread that we
Contain in an out-of-the-way drawer
In our minds but now events are moving
Beyond control with debate arising

Among we siblings over whether she
Is able to be safe inside her home.

I'm getting ahold
of what medicine she needs
at what times and I'm
seeing that she's eating
so order is emerging.

I need to know what and whom I can trust
And I sincerely put faith in people
Until they show me by their behavior
Without question they are untrustworthy

Then I let go of my expectations
Which takes painful practice but I do trust
That when I fold my body into the
Lotus position and meditate that

I will escape for a time the realm of
Human hysteria by attending
To the radical simplicity of
My breath and the beating of my heart which

Remind me that I am only a
Droplet within a cosmic consciousness.

It's manageable
by noticing my breath and
my beating heart to
quell my racing thoughts and to
dwell within simplicity.

A memory of this porch lives in me
Of when it was newly built of lovely
Wood panels and the foldout bed is here
Where Yoshiko and I slept while we were

On vacation in America and
It was the first time for my Japanese
Wife to visit the country and I was
Looking at my hometown and the house where

I grew up and also my Mom and Dad
With fresh appreciative eyes after
Living abroad for several years and now
I'm divorced my Dad has passed and my Mom

Is frail but the optimism of the
Time 30 years ago lives sadly on.

The huge cottonwood
under which I mowed the lawn
as a teenager
was cut down because of
the strike of a lightning bolt.

"I worry . . ." she says as if it were a
Badge of honor and she can't because she's
Busy but something needs doing and so
She recommends that I rush Mom to the

Clinic to have Dr. Wessel check the
Bump on her neck to consider if
A biopsy is necessary as
I hear barely suppressed hysteria

Inside her voice and I do acknowledge
The sincerity and the assistance
My sister's given in looking after
Mom but I do regret her habit of

Running in frenzied circles and then her
Insistence that I run in circles too.

Impassively I
listen imitating as
well as I might
the Rock of Gibraltar as
I refuse to be frazzled.

P.S. There is no bump.

**Things that Happened
At the Poetry Workshop**

    • A guy strode determinedly by in a
Gray- and white-striped T shirt and red sneakers
    • A woman nearby erupted in a
Vituperate rage about something
    • A guy by a trailer was lazily
Putting branches into a woodchipper
    • The East Side Freedom Library built by
Andrew Carnegie was quite imposing
    • The leaves made a lovely shade for us as
We sat in lawn chairs circled on the grass
    • A window washer leisurely plied a
Long-handled squeegee to the church windows
    • I thoroughly enjoyed the relaxing
Ambience of a Saturday morning.

In between each of
the above we read out loud
and silently each
other's poems and then we
traded our commentary.

What I like about writing poetry
Is that I can eliminate so much
Of the clutter in my life by simply
Not including it inside of the words

That I choose to put on paper even
Though it is there fighting for my precious
Attention and energy but instead
I may focus on optimism and

Panache and compose lines of crystalline
Meaning without ambiguity as
I don't demand that my readers perform
Cerebral acrobatics to achieve

Comprehension and I smile picturing
The smile I put on my readers' faces.

Half of the mission
of a life should be to squeeze
frivolity from
conundrums along with the
humdrum preoccupations.

By the time we get to the hind part of
A book of poetry I imagine
You my readers are perhaps a little
Impatient to finish and be done with

Me because I'm like that too even with
Agatha Christie who is as fine a
Writer as could be wished for but may I
Encumber you with a modest pointer?

That the rhymed sonnets are intricate and
Subtle and may be read enjoyably
Over again as there is a game of
Rhyming odd words and half-rhyming going

On that perhaps escaped your notice on
The first harried dashing through the pages.

My unrhymed sonnets
are trifling and frivolous
composed amid the
hurly burly and hysteria
with a gesture of castoff ease.

So simple is William Wordsworth's poem
Of a violet "among untrodden
Ways" hidden by a "mossy stone" and so
Apropos to the "maid" Lucy who

Lived with "very few to love" or "to praise
Her" or to know when "she ceased to be" but
To William Lucy was as "Fair as a
Star" and William uses just a few words

As fitting as an epitaph on a
Gravestone to memorialize his love
And I had quite forgotten his little
Poem until happenstance returned it

To me and I suggest you read it too
In honor of William and of Lucy.

May William and Lucy
be a perennial
memory of a
memory.

Twenty years ago on Tuesday morning
Two highjacked airliners flew into the
World Trade Center and then in a scene of
Horror the two massive towers fell and

Filled the open sky with billowing clouds
Of toxic dust and debris and while the
Heroes of the day the firemen and
Police are as resolute as ever

And America's soldiers are battle-
Scarred and are as disciplined as ever
America's leaders are proving to be
Both arrogant and incompetent and

Unworthy of the sacrifice of those
Who have died in America's defense.

There is bitterness
and ruination in the
affairs of state and
no end to the suffering
of ordinary people.

Among the green leaves
a breeze drops but
a few yellow leaves
keep falling.

—*Tekkan*

Everyday Mind XXIV

The scarlet of the
sugar maples is
the first to pop.

Benji came to the park for our meeting
In a jacket with fabric around his
Neck with jeans and a ball cap and he does
Appear more bundled up which is fitting
As it is September and it's turning
Colder but then I wonder why he is
Wearing sandals without socks and I quiz
Him on his incongruity asking
Wouldn't his mostly bare feet defeat the
Purpose in choosing mostly warmer clothes?
And he remarks that he's stubborn and won't
Give in to the weather yet which is a
Belligerent attitude I share though
He thinks he is sensible — but I don't.

Cold air and bare feet
make my whole body chilly
but Benji may be
different and through force of
will he can stymie the cold.

On my bicycle gravity gets to
Hurt me on the hill to Houlton when I
Take the strain in my anguished breath and I
Expend the strength of body and heart to
Keep my legs going to raise my head to
Glimpse the crest before I lower my eyes
Because it's much easier not to try
To look above and it is better to
Stay in pace with my shadow on the hill
While my silhouette flexes before me
As my vision narrows as I'm going —
Eliminating stray thoughts is a skill
Moving single-pointedly is gutsy
Defeating the hill is satisfying.

Afterward in the
evening gravity gets to
punish me on the
couch as I recline and then
feel the strain of standing up.

Bison gave the Lakota everything
Said elder John Fire Lame Deer — and we used
His hide for our blanket our coat our bed —
Tipis and drums were made of skin — nothing
Was wasted — at night our drums were throbbing
Alive holy — with his stomach we made
Our soup kettle by dropping in a red-
Hot stone — and his skull with the pipe leaning
Against it was our sacred altar — his
Hooves became our rattles and his horns were
Our spoons — his sinews our bowstrings and thread —
His flesh strengthened us — became our flesh — his
Bones we made into knives — and his ribs were
Our children's sleds — and this is what you killed.

The greatest Sioux was
Tatanka Iyotake
Sitting Bull — when you
killed the bison you killed the
wild natural Indian.

I ask a question of a Zen master
"Where is the pathway to liberation?"
The master flips my expectations
He says "everyday mind" is the answer
At first it makes my footsteps easier
As I can make use of my frustrations
I don't have to strain at self-negation
And don't have to rush to get there faster
Ordinary perceptions are all that
I need as long as I'm attending to
What I am thinking — as it's happening —
The clues are here in what I'm looking at
There's nothing special that I have to do
Even mundane chores can be exciting.

The master says it
is outside of words
outside traditions
and there's nothing you
can do to grasp it.

Of course doing sonnets is just a game
That can't be compared with a hunt for truth
And I do sonnets because in my youth
I got caught up in William Shakespeare's fame
But how I'm doing it isn't the same
Because Shakespeare had to be quite a sleuth
With words without dictionaries for proof
Of the rightness of his words and to name
Phenomena with felicity as
He did far surpasses what I can do
And I'm relying on Rhymzone.com
On the Internet which readily has
So many suitable words easy to
Choose from — which I'm doing without a qualm.

I can't imagine
with my sloppy handwriting
using a pen and
relying on memory
to fashion each of my rhymes.

Imagine using a quill pen trying
Not to make any mistakes knowing that
Each page of paper is precious and that
What a waste it would be to be splotching
Its pristine quality by blundering
With ink and what could one do with a splat
But start over again while feeling flat
And then how absolutely frustrating
It would be to be wasting so much time
In repeating stupidly the same chore
Of attempting not to fumble again
And how would it be possible to rhyme
When the handwriting becomes such a bore
And mindless activity is a drain.

Back in the day the
fops paraded about town
wearing rapiers
which perhaps wasn't so good
for handwriting frustration.

When the sun is coming but hasn't yet
Risen over the horizon the trees
Are only black silhouettes and the leaves
Cast a darkness and it is hard to get
A view of details and the yard is set
In gloom and then slowly the shadows ease
And suddenly a wispy cloud is seized
In a pink light and then the grass looks wet
And drops of dew are shining on the hedge
And the needles of a pine are yellow
And swaths of leaves become brilliant with light
And each angle of the shed has an edge
And a few feathery clouds are mellow
And the sun behind the maple is bright.

A flock of tiny
birds flits between a dozen
trees and most of the
leaves are tinged in a slanting
light but there are still shadows.

It's difficult to talk about issues
With people who aren't attending to the
Small details of politics because the
Public rhetoric is just a tissue
Of lies and the reporters often choose
To take sides and so it's hard to find a
Common ground with people who don't have a
Clue when they put so much faith in the news
Which is tragically skewed — and it's tricky
For politicos because they want to
Be aggressive and not be defensive
And they fashion their lies without pity
For anyone they hurt because it's true
Domination is cruelly offensive.

Ordinary and
innocent people would be
abashed to learn how
many of their opinions
are based upon clever lies.

After the many poems I've written
I think it is possible that the point
Of what I'm doing may be out of joint
With you my readers as I've been bitten
By doing Zen by trying to fit in
A yen for liberation — to pinpoint
The moment of freedom in the midpoint
Of "everyday mind" as I believe in
The saying that each of us is Buddha
But we remain ignorant of the fact
So I am trying not to disappoint
You or exhaust you by leading you on a
Goose chase or by awarding you a sack
Of nothing as if it were a viewpoint.

Walking about on
the hunt for poetic
inspiration I've
been looking for freedom
in the writing of poems.

Genghis Khan was a brutal general
Coming from the steppes of Mongolia
He was the opposite of *Siddhartha* —
Was his vicious cavalry temporal?
Were his gory conquests ephemeral?
He wasn't *Avalokitesvara*
Who is a mythical *bodhisattva*
The Khan's ambitions were imperial —
The horse soldiers of Genghis Khan used bows
And arrows to lay waste to more land than
Any other ruler in history
And his clever brutality was so
Calamitous that his memory spans
Millennia in bloody infamy.

Somehow the hunt for
liberation coexists
with a primal lust
for viciousness that appears to
to be inexhaustible.

If you are one of those who don't turn
To a dictionary when they come to
An oddball word then you won't have a clue
About *bodhisattvas* — so why not learn?
It would only take a minute to earn
A propitious bit of wisdom new
To you on which you could happily chew
Over in your head as it's good to yearn
For a wider circumference of knowledge
And you could also easily look up
Avalokitesvara which I know
Is a puzzle to pronounce on the edge
Of absurdity — but why not shape up
Your vocabulary with some gusto?

You may not know that
Avalokitesvara
is an exalted
bodhisattva who has
one thousand busy hands.

When I got to Aldi's grocery store
I discovered that it was a sad day
Because no matter how much I would pay
I couldn't buy the thing that I adore
Because now they don't have it anymore
And there's really nothing that I can say
And why complain when it is just the way
That things are even though it is a bore
As there is a season for everything
And we have to endeavor to let go
Of succulent items on occasion
Otherwise we risk being ding-a-lings
And suffering is part of life — although
Patience becomes part of the equation.

Now I have something
to look forward to as it's
certain in June or
July watermelons will
be available again.

When the full moon is in the morning sky
It looks like a fixture stationary
Beyond the scattered clouds and it's very
Bright and as I'm absorbing the clouds I
Can see that they're transforming on the fly
As wind-blown wisps moving gradually
And I love to give my sight to airy
Sun lit visions because it breaks my ties
To the drama of my human world that
Never seems to cease for me on the ground
When my thoughts race one after another
But the sky shifts about at a pace that
Dissipates urgency and I'm not bound
To fixate on problems and be bothered.

There is nothing in
the sky to grab a hold of
and give context to
the fact the moon is moving
ceaselessly in an orbit.

Fran said that the swallows are mostly gone
Now and I've noticed that too when I'm on
My bike and so many others are on
The move and Fran says that they're being drawn
Southward not by the increasing cold on
The rise or by the darkness coming on
But because the food that they depend on
Becomes scarce in winter and that they're on
The fly at night so we don't see them go
And may not notice their absence — although
Because my head is in the clouds I know
By association of the outflow
Of the songbirds and I'm sad even though
I know that they'll be back next year to woo.

How can chickadees'
spare muscle and bone
sinew and feathers
withstand the cold of
northern winters?

I returned home in the evening and gave
In to the eventuality of
The season as there does come a point of
No return — in spite of my urge to save
Money — what I felt inside was a wave
Of chilly onslaught which I do not love
So I capitulated and I shoved
A little lever to become a slave
To the thermostat and to my furnace
Once again because I am not like my
Kitcat equipped with fur but am truly
A bare creature and my epidermis
Is prone to the shivers — though I may try
To deny it — the cold facts are ugly.

In Minnesota
the temperature is like
a toothache when at
a definite point we know
that things aren't getting better.

Sometimes I don't know why I bother to
Confabulate with words on paper when
I'm confused and don't know how to begin
But once I get going I do get clues
And the writing becomes a rendezvous
Of amusement and worthiness wherein
My words and humor become a linchpin
In revealing to me what I should do
Because things hold together — or they don't —
And I can waste my time asking "Why not?" —
Which I do regretfully — or I can
Simply experiment with words which can't
Hurt me while I frolic with verbal knots —
And I don't think half-rhyming is a sin.

I'm on a quest to
see how much nonsensical
verbiage I can
slather on a page before
you revolt and stop reading.

of

For some reason he chose the title "**of**"
And I don't know what he was thinking of
And perhaps it was because of his love
Of words that he selected a word of
Little significance almost drained of
Worth except to serve the language thereof
As it does so humbly play the role of
A connection between the words above
Its own articulated power of
Description as opposed to "Molotov
Cocktail" which are two exquisite words of
Incandescent quality with much of
The air of urban revolutions of
Fiery history you may have heard of.

My friend Cid Corman
wrote a two-volume set of
poems of over
1,000 pages with the
provocative title "**of**."

My Mom suffered a spasm of the neck
About a month ago and as she is
Eighty-six years old her condition was
Awful because for days she was a wreck
In terrible pain and we rushed to check
At the clinic with a doctor to quiz
Him about the trouble and to get his
Diagnosis/prognosis with the tech
Of ultra-modern pharmacopeia
And we got some pain-soothing medicine
But mostly our task was to provide care
As now we know there's no panacea
And it's helpful to have a regimen
Of watchful care in which we siblings share.

After a month Mom
is almost back to normal
except that she can't
turn her neck to the right and
so she's not able to drive.

I don't know whether she's my girlfriend or
Not but we've spent a lot of time with each
Other and I believe that she's a peach
And I'd really like to open the door
To a deeper relationship before
Something might happen and she's out of reach
And I aim to be playful in my speech
As I really don't want to be a bore
But I'm only meeting her once a week
Usually at a restaurant and
We talk for an hour on the phone at
Five a.m. and I've had more than a peek
Of her person which stimulates my glands —
I am what am and that's a tomcat.

I have the proclivity
And the creativity
To make her giggle
And then to wiggle
With just my verbosity.

It becomes obvious when a girl gets
Under my skin and starts to bother me
When I'm losing sleep and my thoughts aren't free
When I'm not with her and begin to fret
About her and it's difficult to let
Go and I feel my insecurity
And then I question my maturity
And a part of me certainly regrets
Becoming so damn dependent on her
But when I am with her I go out of
My way to make sure she has what she needs
And I'm shocked at what I do on the spur
Of the moment I think because of love
Which isn't gentle but does make me bleed.

When I'm with her in
a group of people whom I
don't know I don't give
a damn about what they think
and I'll look foolish for her.

This kind of love isn't gentle at all
I do regret my insecurity
I don't like manifesting jealousy
And there are days when I'm in a freefall
When I think that she could be my downfall
As she really appears to be carefree
While I don't know how she feels about me
And I get tired of the folderol
Because I suspect that she doesn't feel
Insecure like I do and she isn't
Losing sleep as I am because I do
Worry that loving isn't a big deal
For her and whether it is she doesn't
Show it — leaving me to simmer and stew.

But then there are times
when our words mesh together
so beautifully that
I am exuberant and
I forget all my troubles.

Of course I have to write about it as
I'm doing my gig of "everyday mind"
And I'm working hard at it — in a bind —
Scrounging for topics with razzamatazz
And love is material with pizzazz
And isn't infatuation defined
As what happens when poise is left behind
When I'm seized by unpredictable jazz
And as love has encumbered my life how
Could I have done anything else but
Grapple with it and put it on paper —
To admit that I may be crazy now —
And to make my insanity clear-cut —
Suggesting that love may be a vapor.

The object of my
love is a person with such
gravity that I
became a moon orbiting
her sunny brilliance.

Perhaps you haven't noticed yet but the
Mind is a wild epiphenomenon
That pops into existence carried on
From continuing vibrations of the
Tiny particles following on the
Cosmic cataclysm still going on
That we have named the "Big Bang" that brought on
Everything out of nothing which is a
Strange phenomenon that's hard to put one's
Finger on and appreciate — and then
You may not have noticed that you have no
Control of so many thoughts — which is fun —
When thoughts just pop into existence when
Least expected at a crazy tempo.

Can you say
what your next thought
will be — and how much
trouble it will cause?

I do scribble about "everyday mind"
Because it's a phenomenon that we
All share and is as simple as can be
And it's not at all difficult to find
But I wonder if I've clearly defined
It enough for you to see how easy
It is not to notice its repartee
For everything that happens is aligned
With "everyday mind" and everything in
The world wouldn't even exist without
Its presence and it's more than the ego
As its fine-woven roots are twined within
Cosmic significance despite self-doubt
As it is consciousness both high and low.

It is the unborn
and undying quality
of consciousness that
exists everyday along
with what is ephemeral.

One of my apple trees is losing its
Bark along its west-facing side and I've
Noticed the branches along the west side
Have been barren of leaves and how sad it
Is to observe my tree going to bits
And I suppose that it's destined to die
Perhaps because the summer was so dry
And there's nothing that I can do to fix
The situation — and I remember
Planting this apple tree because of its
Fruit and its blossoms twenty years ago
With my young family at the center
Of my life — and the tree is on the fritz
And the family dispersed a while ago.

I've adopted the
Japanese tendency
for tasting the sad
transitory nature of
life in the blossoming trees.

What would happen if the idea were
Taken seriously that the thing that
Happens suddenly and the person that
Responds are not separate things but are
Only one happening? Would it be far-
Fetched and such a distortion to look at
The doer and the deed as one thing at
The moment — and would you think that's bizarre?
A poem is happening now and words
Are rising to defined prominence from
A jumble of possible words that are
Subjective and would it be so absurd
To think the poet and the words that come
Reflect cosmic connection that's aware?

It's hard not to get
caught in the idea that
the doer makes it
happen and to minimize
what the cosmos is doing.

I've been exploring Agatha Christie
Paperback murder mysteries that are
On my Dad's bookshelves and the pages are
Yellow with age and I love the intrigue
And so I am reading without fatigue
Because the words that she has chosen are
Perfect for the people and times that are
Vanished now and her plots are so twisty
That I never know what's going to happen
And yesterday I saw on the cover
A fingerprint in what I recognized
As printer's ink and so I was saddened
To realize that my Dad had hovered
Over this novel and was mesmerized.

The printing press that
we both operated
became obsolete
and now the room is empty
except for the memories.

I am incurably curious and
Ask myself questions that I can't answer
And I think the cosmos is a dancer
With the earth spinning on its axis and
Orbiting the sun annually and
With the solar system moving faster
Orbiting the Milky Way — and it's queer
That the Milky Way is moving too and
Going even faster moving away
From wherever the Big Bang exploded —
And I want to face in each direction
One after another but I can't say
How to find each direction within mid-
Air — and these become perplexing questions.

At this moment I am
going in four directions
at the same time —
I want to *know*
the direction
of the earth's rotation
the earth's orbit
the solar system's orbit
and the direction
of the Milky Way.

I am conflicted when I gaze at my
Cottonwood on the corner of my yard
Because it continually bombards
The grass with twigs and branches and they lie
There until I pick them up and I sigh
Because it's troublesome and then it's hard
When all the leaves come down without regard
For my schedule which quickly goes awry
But then I see how fitting the bark is
With its deep grooves for the squirrels to grab
Ahold of and to climb and in winter
The tree's unsymmetrical beauty does
Seize my curiosity in the drab
And frigid season that makes me shiver.

The pure yellow of
the leaves in autumn reminds
me that in China
only the Emperor could
wear the color of the sun.

I am as puny as an army ant
And subject to superior power
Earth rotates at 1,000 miles per hour
I can expostulate and I can rant
But I'm not that much quicker than a plant
Earth orbits at 67,000 miles per hour
Maybe I am a walking sunflower
Unaware of gravitational slant
The solar system orbits the Milky
Way at 500,000 miles per hour
And the Milky Way is very weighty
Speeding at 1.3 million miles per hour
So I am barreling that fast too — *whoopee!*
I'm in the belly of cosmic power.

The speed of light is
186,000
miles per second —
is that quicker
than a thought?

Whenever I think about the future
It won't happen like I imagine it
So why worry even a little bit?
But I think I know what's going to occur
And I concoct my plans as I prefer
Manipulating for my benefit
Thinking of scenarios to outwit
Certain people who I want to deter
But with certain problems I do admit
I can't foresee the snares I will incur
With many outcomes that I won't permit
And I am careful but I only spur
Anxiety — which makes me a halfwit —
Whatever I do the future's a blur.

I'm very clever
and have my best interests
in mind so I am
prepared anticipating —
but it won't happen like that.

Rest in Peace Mike Finley

The sorrow of his daughter's death and the
Disappointments of his life tormented
Him but his misfortunes also sweetened
Him giving his curiosity a
Wicked edge and his vitality a
Biting restlessness which I think he used
To drive his intensity which deepened
Him and I guess that he always had a
Sharp and ridiculous kind of humor
But his suffering gave him sympathy
With the many friends whom he got to know
And as he was a great storyteller
I always noticed his sincerity
Which was a quality that made him grow.

He asked me if I
had children and I replied
that yes I did and
he sincerely suggested
that I simply just love them.

I'm at an age when it is typical
To have known many people who have died
And I think it's helped me to decide
How to be sensible and practical
And feel the emptiness of funerals
To sample the emotions that abide
After the ambitions are set aside
To face the fact of the unthinkable
And maybe my friends will die before me
And few will be left to remember me
Perhaps just several of my family
So it's better to drop my vanity
To be as genuine as I can be
And not be angry — and let things be.

My life will have been
mostly a success if at
my passing those who
know me remember my jokes
and I am not a burden.

At Aldi's grocery store the checkout
Clerks are inquisitive and they inquire
Whether I found the things that I require
And I politely say I've looked about
That I've been careful and hunted throughout
And though I did not tire or perspire
There is indeed something that I require —
I'm not irascible and I don't pout
But there's something to find out about as
I couldn't find my favorite zebra
Or the peppered hippopotamus so
I'm glad the clerk inquired of me and was
Hospitable because it's not the law
And their service is better than so-so.

These clerks don't know how
dangerous and inviting
it is to ask an
open-ended question to
a bored individual.

I am a blasé individual
And my job is to observe politics
To study all about their dirty tricks
And every day it is so typical —
Lying and cheating is continual —
I'd enjoy beating them with whips and sticks
As they're no better than blood-sucking ticks —
And I believe I am forgivable
When I am neglecting what I should do —
Instead of working I'm writing sonnets
Making fun of these political creeps —
If you were me wouldn't you do that too?
They think they're special with glamor and glitz
I've no idea of how they can sleep.

Sanctimony and
righteousness are oh so
propitious for
leveraging a useful
topical accusation.

I used to think that rhyming sonnets was
For the birds because it becomes a drag
And I don't want my poetry to sag
Into feckless stupidity because
I force words together and ignore flaws
While I simply enjoy creating gags
And I do admit that I like to brag
Which consecrating a new poem does
But you should picture me with a sly smile
As I imagine you reading my words
After all this is just mindless fooling
Which I could keep repeating by the mile
So don't blame me if you think it's absurd —
You see it's your time that I've been stealing.

Have you wondered what
the expression "for the birds"
actually means?
Does it imply something is
lofty or ridiculous?

Elliptical orbiting seems to be
A motion that the cosmos loves to do
As even the electrons do it too —
There is so much moving that we don't see
When the planets approach their apogee —
Solstice and equinoxes happen too
The cosmos is dancing a whoop-de-do
And I often forget to say *whoopee* —
But when I notice the sugar maples
That turn into the brightest of crimson
Yellow or orange I can't help but mark
The movement of seasons and I'm able
To cherish the quality of the sun
As the difference of the light is stark.

Scientists discovered
that quarks exhibit
either a left- or
right-handed spin.

Sonnets are a Houdini trick with words
Which I used to think was ridiculous
Because the rhyming is superfluous
Flimflam unless I want to be absurd
Turning rhyming couplets into passwords
So my poetry may be frivolous
Though my intentions are meticulous
But I won't let my essence become slurred
And I am writing sonnets because I
Fell in love with them while waiting for a
Train in Amsterdam while passing time with
Shakespeare's complaints about love and I try
To recapture youthful naiveté
By being a preposterous wordsmith.

I combine
sincerity with
play and confusion
circles into clarity.

Shakespeare lathered on the melodrama
Writing monuments of words about love
And such highfalutin fluff is above
My experience — which is of trauma —
So I'm expanding my panorama
By wanting a woman I'm unsure of
That perhaps I should be more careful of
Because in her own words she gave me a
Warning while we were driving together
The other day saying that the worst that
Could happen would be that we would split with
No further communication — and her
Offhanded comment may become a fact
Of life that I will have to contend with.

The bard wrote
140 sonnets
about an affair
offering no
resolution.

Foolish politicians are sometimes said
To have created circumstances by
Their wickedness wherein they have to lie
And keep on lying with increasing dread
Lest their true character be discovered
As the lust for power intensifies
The magnitude of deceit multiplies
And all they can do is to speed ahead
Deceiving themselves with everyone else
As if they are riding a tiger and
Holding on and being carried along
Lest they tumble off and meet the abyss
Of being eaten by the tiger and
That kind of justice is worthy of song.

Are my own
self-deceits
hypnotic illusions
and snares of love
like riding a tiger?

There was the day at the bagel shop where
I met her for breakfast when she saw a
Table of other guys and she said a
Few of them were datable if things were
Different and I suppose that she cares
About me but there was much more than a
Hint of indifference and maybe a
Dosage of cruelty inside of her
Words which was shocking — and on another
Day we arranged to meet again at the
Bagel place and I waited for her but
She didn't come and so I called her number
And she said she changed her plans without a
Reason — and I was upset — but so what?

Yeah! I think I've
written enough love sonnets
to have fulfilled the
tradition so now I'm free
to address other puzzles.

We don't use quill pens and ink and paper
Any more for the writing of poems
But we do have to have a stratagem
And mine is to stimulate a caper
To have fun and be critical later
By all means not to be *ad hominem*
Especially within a requiem
Where I would be an abominator
But it is my game to finagle words
And to fiddle with a catgut line of
Logic well enough to string a reader
Along skirting the edge of the absurd
Perhaps sprinkling a poem with love
Happy to be a communicator.

I would like to leave
readers with the impression
that I've given them a
a series of bonks on the
forehead with a feather.

Whatever there is to awaken to
The masters who have done it do say that
It can't be seized by force of will and that
There's absolutely nothing one can do
To manhandle its arrival and so
I am lost in a labyrinth of what
It means "to do nothing" to be poised at
A point that only breathing is what I do
And even that is doing something a bit
More than not doing anything as my
Mind is incubating a mess of thoughts
No matter how quietly I can sit
And I'm absorbing so much with my eyes
And with a line of geese I do get caught.

Liberation is
a puzzle as the masters
say the happening
is outside of traditions
and words cannot capture it.

There are so many things to think about
And most of them are just nagging details
As I would like to boost my monthly sales —
I'd like to have fame and money and clout —
Occasional loneliness makes me pout —
Could I be a sailor unfurling sails?
Could I satisfy myself spotting whales?
And how often would I spot a whale spout?
My energy goes into managing
My house and when there are unusual
Disturbances I have to check it out
And yesterday Kitcat was galloping
About and then I heard a strange jostle
And a tapping sound to find out about —
Curiosity is stimulating.

Kitcat jostled the
door from the inside of
the cupboard above
and behind the top of
the refrigerator.

He's a creature of curiosity
And I have underestimated him
Because he can be a creature of whim
Scampering in fits of velocity
Showing animal grandiosity
Which could imply that he's a little dim
But he's very clever with his forelimbs
And surprises me with dexterity
As every morning he waits for me to
Brush him and when I'm through I put the brush
On the floor and he seizes the brush and
Turns it upward and he endeavors to
Brush his furry face himself in a rush
And it's almost as if his paws were hands.

I thought that Kitcat
was only able to brush
one side of his face —
then I saw him turn about
and he brushed the other side!

It happened again at the grocery
Store that another checkout clerk inquired
If I had found the things that I required
And once again I said I didn't see
Just where the hippopotamus could be
And again I saw that I inspired
The disorientation I desired
Which I can use to write my poetry
And then I saw the previous girl and
I told her about my caper and asked
If she wanted to hear my poetry
About herself zebras and hippos and
She did and so we moved off to the side
Where I could become a luminary.

In a corner at
the front of Aldi's I
read my doggerel
about my earnest search for
zebras and peppered hippos.

The maple trees in Japan grow tiny
Leaves that turn a lovely shade of crimson
That I anticipated in autumn
And like the plum blossoms and cherry trees
They are celebrated by Japanese
And over the years I have taken on
Rituals and I am depending on
A mysterious sensibility
To mark the poignant unexplainable
Beauty blossoming and passing every
Season by writing poetry that shows
My appreciation for the maple
Trees that turn such lovely colors every
Autumn on the verge of winter shadows.

The *momiji* trees
are pronounced "momeegee" in
Japanese and once
one has seen them
one always remembers them.

I can't imagine William Wordsworth or
John Keats using the topics that I do
And also worthy Aristotle too
Would object and perhaps even abhor
The déclassé subjects that I adore
But I'm not a fool and I've thought it through
Because "everyday mind" is what I do
Which tells me there's no reason to be bored
With ordinary activity so
Three times a week I stand like a silver-
Back gorilla and heave a 100-
Pound dumbbell up and down and I can go
Very fast because I'm a believer
In exercise — and I'm not an egghead.

I am repeating
a pattern of lines and rhymes
that poets have used
for centuries for fun and
why not be innovative?

The clouds move at a gentle pace across
The sky and every season takes some time
To reach fruition and it's a pastime
Of mine to note the continual loss
Of the autumn leaves that I see are tossed
In the blusters of the wind and sometimes
They fall in batches and at other times
They waft and spiral by themselves and cross
My sight which I savor with a joyful
Melancholy — a sad festival — a
Month of dissolving when the leaves come down
And winter soon arrives and the cheerful
Leftover brilliance of the sun in the
Colors of the leaves lies drab on the ground.

Overcast days and
sharp winds howling through
the barren branches
have about them a bleak
and austere kind of beauty.

I do struggle to meet people where they
Are as I understand that they differ
From me as there are so many fissures
And difficulties getting in the way
Subtle and brutal leading us astray
As if differences were like scissors
Separating us as disbelievers
But we could talk on a happier day
As modern life in America is
Divided by ideological
Poison hyped by the mass broadcasting of
Continual accusation that does
Its best to foster pathological
Hatred — the polar opposite of love.

Differences of
race gender ethnicity
are so needlessly
exaggerated and are
slyly exacerbated.

I knew an intellectual guy who
Was an executive at a think tank
In Washington D.C. with so much swank
One had to have connections to get through
His layers of protection and I knew
Him partially and he wasn't a crank
And he well deserved the highest of ranks
Among thoughtful guys one could bump into
But only in his obituary
Did I discover his admiration
For hippopotami which he expressed
With all sorts of hippopotamus toys
And with obsessional jubilation
Which was not at all what I expected.

I can see that a
hippopotamus is an
ebullient mixture
of weighty pomposity
and impetuosity.

I don't mind being among people who
Have opinions and expectations that
Are opposed to mine but if they are at
Odds with me I'd like to be able to
Talk it through but so often now it's true
It's very difficult to arrive at
A place of neutral ground so to get at
The pivotal issues I look for clues
For flexibility grace and humor
Because I'd enjoy a healthy debate
And I am eager to learn something new
But political divisions are sour
And society is poisoned with hate
So being circumspect is what I do.

Being trapped in the
same room with my poetry
political and
Buddhist friends would become a
delicate balancing act.

If I were to say nothing sensible then I could
Avoid the trap of becoming preachy
And part of me thinks it would be peachy
To publish my books *without words* which would
Be a conundrum to my readers which could
Lead them to believe they were terribly
Cheated so I could be adorably
Quizzical and speculate that we should
Not play the game of believing that we
Ourselves are more tolerant and more
Broadminded than you other people are
As we wallow in our humility
But then I would risk becoming a bore
And whatever I say would seem bizarre.

An empty page
is empty of ideas
and flavorless.

Trimming about the rose bush I got a
Splinter imbedded in my thumb which I
Didn't notice while working to apply
The hedge cutter to daylilies and the
Hostas cluttering the yard which is a
Fall ritual wherein I bend my thighs
And spine to level the slicing blade by
The ground and then to rake and gather the
Leaves I straighten my back not noticing
The unusual strain on my body
And this year I could just pull on most of
The plants and they detached with my yanking
Which was easier than I thought it'd be —
To be done was what I was thinking of.

Leaves are in bags
a splinter's in my thumb
and I didn't notice pain
until I stood and walked.

My friend Jason the ecologist took
Issue with my saying that the trees are
Unsymmetrical pointing out that they're
More exquisitely balanced than they look
Otherwise they'd collapse when they are shook
By the wrenching of the winds and as far
As the spreading branches go they too are
Balanced by the displacement of their roots
So even though there's not a straight line or
A perfect curving form to be observed
There's a subtle composition of poise
Supporting every twist and crook before
The buds of the leaves are prepared to spread
In an epitome of equipoise.

The trees harmonize
with the rotation of the
earth synthesize
with the orbit of the earth
and with the strength of the sun.

Modern people are sophisticated
And with mathematically verified facts
We comprehend both galaxies and quarks
Our disproven theories are updated
Conflicting paradigms are debated
We measure our land with accurate maps
And with nanotechnology perhaps
Utopia is anticipated
While I'm watching the sun as it's rising
Doing my best to imagine that I
Can sense the movement of the earth
That I can feel the horizon moving
And can know the protection of the sky
As if this day were a glorious birth.

It's easier to
notice the pulsation of
my blood and heart and
the swelling the pause and the
dissipation of my breath.

On the corner of my property there
Stands a gargantuan cottonwood and
Now that I've disposed of the hostas and
Daylilies I have to wait and to bear
The dread of the labor to come — to fare
As well as I can — when I take in hand
My rake and lawn bags — when I stand and bend
Shoving the leaves into bags with the flair
That I'm accustomed to — but now I have
To watch and to wait as some of the leaves
Are the brightest of yellow and some are
Pristine green and it is tricky to stave
Off my dread as part of me really seethes —
Which I know to you may appear bizarre.

I bend over and
straighten up for many long
hours and afterward
for several days — because I'm
sore — I waddle like a duck.

Oh! what the tricky rosebush did to me
I thought that I had a thorn in my thumb
Though the day I got it my thumb was numb —
I do not indulge in hyperbole
What the rosebush did was a travesty —
I knew where my prickly thumb came from
I'm really quite clever — I am not dumb —
But I didn't see the reality
There wasn't only one thorn inside my
Thumb but three and so because my thumb was
Numb it took several days to see the truth
Whereupon I seized my tweezers to pry
Them out but I got only two because
Life is difficult — and also uncouth.

The leftover thorn
is there in the middle of
my thumb and I can't
retrieve it and it remains
a nasty provocation.

The leaves are descending gradually
And the forms of the trees are apparent
Their gesturing branches are transparent
The season displays a poignant irony
The way of the world is polarity
Summer days were sweltering — now they aren't —
Nothing upon the earth is permanent
Winter is a time of austerity
But how strange it is that before the leaves
Fall off they turn into the most brilliant
Of colors worthy of jubilation
Before the onset of a winter freeze
And to me the autumn leaves represent
A brief expression of exultation.

Who is it that cares
that everywhere on the
earth rainbow colors
will burst into expression
and then suddenly dissolve?

I thought that I was through with her and then
She called and apologized giving me
A story about being suddenly
Despondent and full of self-revulsion
And when that happens there's a compulsion
To sympathize with female company
She said and she called Donna and Sherry
And they went shopping and later on when
She realized that she left me hanging
Waiting for her she said she was sorry
And she wants me to forgive her again
As this is a time when she is hurting
And she's not angry at men — like Sherry —
And she knows that I understand her pain.

I marvel at how
she maneuvers me into
a position where
she neglects me and then she
plays upon my sympathy.

I haven't been angry with her after
All the things she's put me through — at least not
In her presence — but she's tied me in knots
Of frustration which I haven't shown her
And she's very difficult and she spurs
My perplexity now that I am caught
Between attraction and being distraught
Which I cannot let happen forever
Because I'm waking up in the middle
Of the night unable to quiet or
Divert my mind from her and getting up
Doing Zen still leaves me in a muddle
Which means that I have to do something or
Else go on being nervy and screwed up.

I had a taste of
being relieved of tension
and uncertainty
so maybe I can try some
purposeful indifference.

I can see how the monks of Asia would
Separate themselves from the tangles of
Ordinary life like romantic love
Because it's much easier and how could
One follow the allure of womanhood
And liberation also — so full of
Conflicting perplexities are both of
These paths — and yet I think it would be good
In each case if I could learn to relax
When I would like to — and when I need to —
Because so often my emotions run
Away with me inflicting painful cracks
In my composure and knowing what to
Do is easier when I'm having fun.

Surely with either
romantic connection
or a Buddha kind of
of liberation things would
come easier with a smile.

Rhyming sonnets is only a game that
I play and in choosing my words I make
A spontaneous bet and so I take
A real risk with my time and effort that
I can find a harmonious word that
Rhymes and that also pleases for the sake
Of rhythm and sense as it's a mistake
To focus narrowly and to fall flat
With the poem's overall impact as
Reciting a poem is like telling
A joke and if the punchline doesn't work
If there isn't any razzamatazz
And then if I look like a ding-a-ling
My handiwork fails — and I am a jerk.

There is such fun in
the spontaneity of
seizing on a word
and mixing it with other
words to make a quirky joke.

At the top of an ash tree I saw a
Couple of crows and the leaves were down at
The very top but were holding on at
The middle and the crows perched apart a
Little distance silently and then the
Crow on the right bobbed and cawed and then the
Other bobbed and cawed in a manner that
Suggested they were irritated at
Each other tangled in some sort of a
Disagreement and were sniping at one
Another in the way that couples do
And I thought what a dreary scene it is
And how powerful it is when one shuns
The other — and even animals do
It too — and how depressing it all is.

After a passage
of silence and sniping the crows
departed and flew —
together — leaving the tree
to shed its remaining leaves.

I am going on with the idea
That I have my sensual faculties
And my various attitudes and these
Are my determining phenomena
And — because of my dipsomania —
I believe that I can't do as I please
Can't indulge every urge that I am seized
By and if there is a panacea
It's what I can do with my attitude
And I realize I can't wrench myself
Into a better way of feeling but
That I can with a practiced latitude
Let go — as any emotion in itself
Is fleeting and need not become a rut.

If I'm able to
gently coexist with my
perplexities and
frustrations they will simply
dissolve — eventually.

Very often with groups I've been part of
It seems I'm on the outside looking in
And emotions arise that are akin
To aversion with the loneliness of
Being apart and with the confusion of
What to do to quell disruption within
That leads me to self-justification —
When what I want is acceptance and love —
But it does me no good to run away
From such puzzles and I think that it's good
Practice to see what happens over time
To discover whether there comes a way
For harmony to arise — so it would
Be best to be patient in the meantime.

I do have to live
with painful paradoxes
with abiding faith
that I don't have to impose
a forceful resolution.

You may have noticed that I am seeking
Enlightenment by writing poetry
Which maybe is conceited lunacy
As I'm taking pleasure in exploring
Sensuality and in detailing
Ordinary events with clarity
Fixing on the potentiality
That happenstance may be conspiring
With way-seeking mind and I admit I
Can't grasp liberation by force of will
And the harder I try the less likely
I am to succeed — but shouldn't I try
As there is a chance? And maybe I will
Grasp what can't be grasped — at least consciously.

I would like to be
surprised by events into
a revelation
so I'm patiently waiting
and expecting a surprise.

The great gift of Sunday is that I don't
Have to do anything that's scripted by
My livelihood and that I set aside
Regular exercise and I don't
Feel guilty about it because I won't
Let my morning relaxation go by
Without easeful meditation to ply
Thoughts to carefree exploration so it's
Propitious to sit and linger at
My keyboard looking outside the window
As I am fishing in the air for words
With open childlike expectation that
If I wait — even though I don't know how —
Cheerful exuberance comes with my words.

Once I've exhausted
my perceptive energy
my satisfaction
allows me to do household
chores with a happy éclat.

I could be expending effort building
An intellectual superstructure
Weaving philosophical contexture
With metaphorical might resembling
A Gothic cathedral of soaring
Thought anchoring objective conjecture
With flying buttresses as a lecture
Of perfectibility humoring
My conceit with a lofty angled vault
Raised above an expansive lonely nave
Exquisitely enlightened with stained glass
Consistently eliminating faults
Believing myself to be very brave
Becoming an intolerable ass.

I can't live without
a reliable point of
view and while it's good
to be consistent I know
my thoughts are perishable.

I don't have or want a publisher
As I am publishing my books online
And edit exhaustively every line
Rereading every page five times over
And I am determined to do over
Any defective poem taking time
Thinking that any mistake is a sign
Of carelessness and so I look over
My books when they arrive and yesterday
While flipping through the pages I noticed
That one poem was a line space too high
On the page and saw I was betrayed
With a slighting of my *magnum opus*
By a laxity that escaped my eye.

However much I
finagle whatever I
do there seems to come
a moment when a puncture
lets air out of my balloon.

I wonder if a repeated pattern
Of words for example rhyming sonnets
Has intrinsic value or whether it
Is just an ego-based foolish concern
As a sassy display of skill to turn
A phrase in any direction to fit
The predetermined form showing off wit
Which at bottom is about self-concern
But I get bored easily and don't want
To write about the same things over and
Over and to keep going I want to
Answer questions and I don't want to flaunt
Verbal dexterity uselessly and
There is always more exploring to do.

I want to bump up
against the vague edge of the
inexpressible
and for that I'm going to need
much verbal dexterity.

A group of us have come to Pioneer
Park for a gathering which overlooks
The river valley with the dawn in flux
With light on the verge ready to appear
As the beauty of the day is austere
As the season is approaching a crux
Growing colder and darker in redux
Of a seemingly barren season near
Again but we have a portable fire
And we each have a time to say our piece
About experience not feeling drear
In our hearts and our meeting does inspire
A satisfying talk that does bring peace
That gives to the season a certain cheer.

A guy lingers on
the edge of tears wanting
not to break down
talking about memories
of deer hunting with his dad.

When I meditate I make an oval
With the fingers of my hands which rest on
My lap and sometimes I will dwell upon
The oval of my hands as a focal
Point and as my body is immobile
My hands are an epiphenomenon
And my whole consciousness is resting on
The oval space within my hands and so all
My thoughts are arising within my hands
And I hold the force of my life the flow
Of my energy in my hands the fire
Of my attention rests in my hands and
The beating of my heart and the bellows
Of my breath feed the air to my bonfire.

When I finish with
meditation and I move
about doing my
business I have a buffer
between me and disturbance.

The cottonwood on the corner of my
Property is a power unmindful
Of my preferences and I am fretful
Of the coming cold and every year I
Do try to mulch or to bag the entire
Dispensation of all its leaves careful
To finish before the snow comes grateful
To have my yard looking tidy so I
Don't have to do an autumn chore in the
Spring so that I watch the days go by and
I see and wait for the yellow leaves to
Fall but there is nothing to do in the
Meantime but to quell my impatience and
Linger until the heaps of leaves accrue.

The yellow flags of
cottonwood leaves turn and
reflect leftover
summer sunshine and once they
go the landscape becomes drab.

OK I have reached the point in the book
Where I am going to dispense with rhymes at
Least at the end of my lines but I'll be
Counting syllables and measuring the

Length of my lines and the task of writing
Remains the same that is to compose the
Right words in the correct order without
Wasting space on useless words that are there

Only to make a ten-syllable line
With the overall purpose of leading
Up to an ending that is worthy of
The writing and the reading of it for

Otherwise I'd let you down and you could
Languish in a dystopian cosmos.

The world is pregnant
and poignant with meaning and
I hope some of it
emerges in word tracery
upon these empty pages.

My elderly Mom is assailed by a
Telephone fraudster who frightens her with
His claims of government authority
Declaring her Social Security

Number is compromised and that to catch
The thief she needs to go to Walmart and
Walgreens and to buy $500
Gift cards and so by reading the number

On the back of the card to the caller
She could be protected from this scumbag
Which is a damnable lie repeated
By this insolent slimebag ensconced in

A lair somewhere in America who
Preys on the fears of the elderly.

Disconnecting my
mother from the phone is not
a solution but
persuading her to hang up
ferociously is helpful.

Across the river valley in plain sight
From Pioneer Park there stands a tower
With antennae for cell phone coverage
And before dawn lights are blinking on the

Tower a glowing lovely scarlet flash
Timed with intervals calculated I
Am sure to catch the attention of a
Nighttime pilot and everything about

The tower is a technical achievement
Of the modern age but in the darkness
I am able to gaze at the winking
Light with childlike rapture that thrills with such

Simple delight in the beauty of things
Apart from my dull rationality.

Down the valley and
two miles away the Crossing
Bridge is festooned with
emerald and ruby winking
lights shining upon water.

It's in our literature and is part
Of our lore that we compulsive drunks will
"Intuitively know how to handle
Situations which used to baffle us"

After we've been revived enough for the
Anesthetized fog of euphoria
And of despair and then of hangovers
To have dissipated and then even

Into sobriety the tangle of
Emotion that fuels a drunk must be faced
And allowed to dissipate after which
The frustrated and agonized love that

Lies buried within us for many years
Finds enough freedom for its expression.

The expression of
loving understanding we
see and hear in
our faces and our voices
is what we give each other.

On any day I have only to look
Up from my keyboard while I am busy
Collecting my thoughts to observe through the
Window that on certain days the sky is

Heavy with clouds casting a gloom upon
The earth and on other days a few clouds
Will be moving sometimes to the south or
To the north with a unique difference

Of touch every day and today there are
Very few clouds and the remaining leaves
Are bright with yellow light and feathery
Wisps of the clouds are speeding southward with

An awe-inspiring drama as I
Can see their brilliant whiteness transforming.

They lead me to think
of the sail-rigged and sleekly
designed clippers full
of lusty sailors plying
skills on the swelling ocean.

I ruined my handwriting doing a
Lengthy freshman essay in college by
Writing in a rush compulsively as
I struggled to keep up with the blasts of

My thoughts and ever since then even though
I try to be careful I am sloppy
So it's good to use a computer for
Poetry and now I sit and dwell with

Thoughts before I strike a key as I am
Not scattershot anymore but I do
Have to use a pen when thanking people
For their donations to my business and

Handwriting is a peculiar kind of
Labor with such convulsive hand fatigue.

Occasionally
I exert effort to write
every letter of
"Parkway" but usually
I just scrawl "Pkwy."

Aristotle preferred elevated
Topics for poetry and so I guess
He'd take a low opinion of my lines
As I take an interest in the little

Red squirrel that runs along the top of
The white fence in the yard outside of the
Window and I'd like you my reader to
Watch with me with simple pleasure as the

Squirrel follows the curving pattern of
The fence scampering up and down stopping
And resuming turning a corner and
Disappearing behind a shed and with

Me perhaps you may lighten your mood and
Escape the nonsense you were thinking of.

Observation of
ordinary happenings
may well become a
pleasurable relief from
embroiled preoccupation.

I was new to the poetry reading
Scene and he had made an impression on
Me as being a poet who knew what he
Was doing so I summoned my courage

And laid before him the seven books that
I self-published and he was courteous
And kindly praised my daughter's cover art
Which gave the books harmonious appeal

He said but then he remarked that it's hard
For poets and that we poets often
Can't even give our work away and I
Believe that night he recognized in me

The hungering ambition to become
Through force of will somebody important.

At our monthly show
the "Barbaric Yelp" on a
depressing winter
night Mike Finley was hurting
from chemotherapy

I left the "Barbaric Yelp" that gloomy
Night feeling like an outcast which I'm sure
Was not Mike's intention and then I bumped
Into him at many venues about

The Twin Cities where he introduced me
To his friends and he gave me a welcome
Access to his home his conversation
His experience — with the lessons learned —

And as one of his friends I was grateful
To shelter under the umbrella of
His compassion which he spread above the
Many people whom he got to know and

Mike has served us as a guide because
He had suffered and rejoiced so deeply.

Many friends at his
memorial told stories
of youthful ribald
explosive optimistic
and verbal exuberance.

A friend of mine related how he liked
The female attention he received from
The young nurses who cared for him in the
Hospital after colon surgery

And he reminisced about his father
On his deathbed in the hospital when
His Dad confided that even on the
Threshold of death he was attracted to

The fetching young nurses about him as
If he were a 30-year-old able
To seek a woman again and I groaned
With the recognition that as long as

My heart circulates blood I will never
Be free of the desire for women.

I could believe that
this overwhelming yearning
is an affliction
or that it's God's blessing but
I can't be indifferent.

The sparrows are playing flitting between
Several trees as a roving flock and
They dip in flight and rise before they perch
And they turn suddenly in the air toward

Another tree and they're not flying in
Formation purposely as the geese do
But are frolicking restlessly at ease
Hopping and perhaps hiding however

Temporarily in the remaining
Foliage and the sparrows aren't giving
Any thought to their acrobatics as
Nothing could be easier than flight and

Busybody scavenging in a group
For them as they move to different trees.

They rise together
above the trees swerving
and darting away
leaving the increasingly
bare branches to twig gestures.

I turn the corner in my car and see
The oak trees that are three blocks ahead that
Mark the place on the street across from my
Office which is a view embedded in

My daily routine hardly worthy of
Notice yet the oaks which are the last of
The trees to shed their leaves are well into
Autumn and the leaves are shining in a

Poignant red in the morning light that brings
To mind a morning of the previous
Winter of the sight of frost-encrusted
Bare branches glowing within an orange

Brilliance transiently before the sun
Moved on and then the light dissipated.

The distinctiveness
of oak leaves and oak branches
do assert themselves
periodically in my
mind in my yearly routine.

For 25 years I've made disposing
Of the cottonwood leaves that fall on my
Yard a much bigger chore than it needed
To be by waiting until all the leaves

Were down thinking as I did that it is
Better to do all the work at once and
Be done with it but this year I have mulched
With the mower as leaves landed over

Several days and they didn't have the
Time to accumulate in odd places
On the patio and betwixt the house
And garage so I didn't rake so much

So that I didn't have to bend over
To bag the leaves which does make me so sore.

Only in retrospect
after blundering into
different ways did
it emerge that it's not the
time but the strain that matters.

As I was removing my friend River's
Wheelchair from the trunk of my car a round
Blue bottle of bug spray fell from a bag
That was slung between the handles of the

Chair and it hit the asphalt plopped and broke
Into shards of glass that scattered about
And River had forgotten about it
And didn't mind its loss and I knelt to

Observe the variously sized and sharp
Pointed bits and with the rounded tips of
My fingers I collected the larger
Pieces and placed them on a little wall

And then being delicate I lifted
Tiny shards and put them into my palm.

I collected the
shattered bottle in one
hand and dropped it in
a dumpster nearby without
slicing or pricking fingers.

I try not to think about it because
Looking for it hinders the happening
But the shock of the breaking of the blue
Glass bottle may be a symbol of the

Moment when delusion vanishes and
A realization of reality
Arrives and the body and mind are thrown
Off and Buddhist enlightenment is in

Hand but that didn't occur for me — much
To my disappointment — so I did the
Essential thing that I could do which was
To patiently and to wholeheartedly

Collect the sharp bits — careful not to pierce
My fingertips — not to puncture my palm.

As I understand
it even the slightest thought
embedded in my
mind — that I have to grasp it —
will prevent liberation.

I would like you my reader to get my
Metaphors with alacrity without
Having to make vague guesses as it is
My gig to look for extraordinary

Ridiculous insight in everyday
Things or — in other words — ordinary
Magic and so I should warn people and
Friends that I'm literal when putting words

Together and if you live within the
Circumference of my consciousness then
There's a possibility that you will
Become an epiphenomenon — that

What you do may be memorialized —
Because I'm looking for material.

With the exception
of a girlfriend on the verge
of becoming an
ex-girlfriend most people don't
know that I am watching them.

If you have a hankering for putting
Words on paper maybe for reasons
You don't yet understand knowing only
That it's exciting to express yourself

To clarify what's important or to
Uncover sly emotions disguising
Genuine emotions or that you have
Stumbled on the secret — that the act of

Writing brings out buried treasure that you
Could find in no other way — if these things
Are true for you then you should create a
Sanctuary in the day for writing

And arrange your routine so that you are
Most awake and alive during that time.

If you have done so
much as to have established
a sanctuary
then the writing becomes a
habit not easy to quit.

Imagine who is reading the writing
Even though at the moment it may be
True as Mike Finley said that poets can't
Give their work away — imagine that the

White page with your words is touching the thoughts
Of someone who's open and eager to
Be a partner — maybe not indulgent of
Your self-pity moroseness — but yet one

Who is not as harshly critical of
You as you often are of yourself — and
Believe that the one you are writing for
Comprehends admires and loves you — and

If you can do that then the words will find
Harmony and you will become happy.

Imagination
can transform the writer's fear
of the empty page
into an unshakable
ever-present companion.

Gripping twisting and pulling with enough
Pressure to accomplish my purpose is
What I sometimes have to do in the course
Of using tools and getting things done and

I'm focusing strength and thinking only
Of results and at other times I am
Striking the keys of the keyboard watching
Letters emerging in rows on a screen

And my fingers are disciplined with years
Of training and are invisible to
Me in a perfunctory way of thought
But I'd like to explore you with touching

Holding and caressing delicately
Consciously with the tips of my fingers.

As if they were the
hands of a child again I'd
like to explore with
you exquisite textures with
loving receptivity.

It is nice to have a garage for a
Car when the first frost of the year sticks to
The windshields of the exposed cars and has
To be scraped off with an edged tool with strength

As I don't have to do that anymore
But I remember the years when I gave
Space to my then-wife for her car and the
Memory is sweetly regretful that

No matter our one-time intentions we
Are better off apart as I see the
Roofs of houses coated in the frost and
The cold of the air penetrates my lungs

And breathing is a little burdensome
As I wait for warmth from the car's heater.

It is nice to have
someone to make such little
sacrifices for
and in their absence the good
deeds done are sweetly missed.

If I keep my eyes open the lag of
A season can take my breath away as
The calendar days go by and I see
The daily demarcations pass in a

Gradual sinking of temperature
In the slow emergence with touches of
Color in the leaves in the selection
Of the heavier clothes that I wear but

I'm watching the trees outside the window
In the absence of a wind dropping their
Leaves fluttering straight down by the hundreds
At a steady pace and in the little

Time it takes to assemble these words the
Stark aspect of the bare branches appears.

Suddenly squirrels
have nowhere to hide and the
valley beyond the
homes and trees is visible
and will be for the winter.

There is the turn every day when I'm done
With the poetry preceded by the
Meditation informed by a hunt for
Liberation when I attend again

To the daily news as a partisan
And because I've been doing this for a
While I can gauge the predatory moves
The dishonesty of political

Talk and the contempt propelling so much
And I believe the world is better off
Because I do political writing
Wherein aggression is expected and

Rewarded — but at the same time I am
Balanced with roots in the ethereal.

Oppression is a
fact counterbalanced by
little expressions
of love persisting throughout
redeeming our intentions.

Fortunately — I have my wits about
Me so that I can cruise smoothly into the
Future while satisfied imagining
What it will be like luxuriating

Rehearsing memories being able
To cherish productive years relishing
Well-earned pride in a compendium of
Poetry wherein reading each of my

Poems will recall to me moments of
Happy exploration involving a
Web of circumstances and connections
And companions wherein I will need to

Overlook the maladroit expressions
That eluded my proofreaders and me.

A sour thought intrudes
reminding me that
whatever I think
will happen — it won't
happen like that.

It has happened so frequently once I've
Confirmed a recognizable profile
Of a female who lives overseas as
A Facebook friend that she encumbers me

With text messages initiating
A whirlwind romance professing as she
Does that she's been treated horribly and
She wants sincerity integrity

And love and she offers fetching photos
Of herself gorgeous and decades younger
Than me and she eagerly awaits my
Response ensnaring me in dialogue

Devolving perhaps to impatience with
My hesitancy to send over money.

Who's titillating whom?
as usually I don't
allow the game to
start as the question becomes
who will be frustrating whom?

The scarlet maple
leaves are grounded — the sun
crests the horizon.

—*Tekkan*

Everyday Mind XXV

Like all the trees
this maple is bare again —
the sky is white.

The truck's engine is roaring up the hill
Filling the morning air with commotion
A consequence of its locomotion
And I appreciate it with good will
Admitting that it's giving me a thrill
Thinking about the driver's devotion
The selfless service of his emotion
His destination being the landfill
As the truck is serving society
By picking up and hauling away a
Week's accumulation of garbage
The effluvium of technology
As it is a necessary and a
Helpful ennobling kind of cartage.

Conversation with
the average garbage truck
driver would be
better than that of a
typical politician.

There is a bush still holding on to its
Leaves right next to Cub Foods where I hear a
Bevy of tiny birds engaged in a
Twittering fit that's not even a bit
Self-conscious as I approach and they get
Quiet as I stand — and then I go a
Little way away and wait — and then the
Racket starts again sounding like half-wit
Commentary — so once more I creep near
And quickly a silence ensues again
But soon there comes a sniping here and there
And I really do think the little dears
Are upset with me and are making it plain
They want privacy and don't want me here.

I think this is the
reincarnated spirit
of a gossip who's
been disembodied into
separated synapses.

I've been thinking about my dignity
Because it often is about the size
Of attendance and I want to apprise
Myself of the best time auspiciously
For me to kick the bucket skillfully
With consideration to maximize
My funeral and not to minimize
The recitation of the litany
Of my accomplishments and I'd like to
Be sure that the story of my travels
And of my publications is told and
I'd like people to have a clear-cut view
Of my selflessness and of the travails
Of my entire life that weren't bland.

Perhaps the crematory
Would be most laudatory
So fling my ashes
In ocean splashes
And be celebratory.

Of course there wouldn't be much benefit
To having a ceremony while not
Enjoying it so I've given some thought
To faking my death writing my obit
Hosting my funeral where I could sit
In disguise among the entire lot
Of my acquaintance to see how distraught
They were and I certainly do admit
That I'm being quite melodramatic
But I'm curious about what they would
Say about me and afterward I'd just
Remark that there was some kind of mistake
Or misunderstanding and then I could
Say the newspapers aren't worthy of trust.

It's not about vanity
Or about my sanity
I'm not bitter
I could live better —
Improve my humanity.

I like to capture the moments of change
In the seasons and the predominance
Of the bare branches — and the somnolence
Of the trees arriving again feels strange —
And the appearance of snow helps to gauge
The sudden shift before my consciousness
Adjusts — as it is the coincidence
Of my watchful and considerate age
That I notice when most of the trees are
Stark and the snow is coating the branches
For the first time this year — as I have seen
This sight under a white sky that is far
Above for decades and today it is
Clear the impact of the branches is keen.

Branches are so
weirdly
explosively
gesturing and yet
they are dormant.

I am like the barn owl gripping a branch
In the woods on the verge of the setting
Sun meditative freezing and hunkering
Down and I am summoning strength to stanch
My dreary thoughts that like an avalanche
Are oppressing and perpetuating
A sense of impending gloom including
A hint of doom — and as winter blanches
The color from the earth so does the cold
Stiffen and sober me reminding me
That there are seasons of difficulty
That I can bolster myself and be bold
And that poised relaxation is the key
To happiness amid austerity.

The barn owl grips a
branch in the gathering gloom
patiently waiting
in the circumference of the
forest for the time to pounce.

How often does it happen that as I'm
Typing poems looking out my window
Experimenting with snappy lingo
That a chickadee appears passing time
On the hedge outside looking like a mime
Of joy hopping and flitting even though
The air enveloping him is below
Zero and so he embodies a chime
With winter and one might even say that
He rhymes with the cold even though he is
The slightest of creatures composed only
Of bone sinew and muscle without fat
Epitomizing effervescent whiz
Gamboling with frolicsome energy.

If only I could
be as frolicsome and spry
as a chickadee
amid the gloom of winter
my thoughts would be whimsical.

Sooner or later I am going to stop
Because writing sonnets isn't easy
And I wouldn't say that I am lazy
But I do have to write my agitprop
As political hijinks are nonstop
The quality of my thoughts is hazy
I'm thinking in rhymes and that's just crazy
It is true that every rhyme is a prop
Which I hope really pops and doesn't flop
Which truthfully serves as a sop to my
Ego which plays and habitually
Mops my insecurity on the hop
With my lines of nonsense that do not lie
That may well approximate poetry.

I do need some scrutiny
Of my insecurity
Rhyming is crazy
And makes me lazy
I'd rather have sanity.

Relaxation is very important —
If I could do it when I needed to
There'd be little else that I'd have to do
As I wouldn't be pensive or mordant
All my afflictions would be impotent
Insecurity wouldn't stick like glue
And whatever comes I could see it through
I'd be decisive — not ambivalent —
I'd like to be wholehearted while letting
Go of results so I wouldn't worry
But I can't do that very well and so
Now I am wholeheartedly accepting
My unquenchable insecurity —
Trying to relax — so it doesn't grow.

I have to relax
with however much of my
insecurity
there is at the moment and
there's nothing else to do.

Did you ever make a hideous face
With friends as a child — just being funny?
Today is laughing and smiling easy?
We humans communicate face to face
We have ample ability to grace
Our friends with affectionate repartee
Swapping carefree facial hyperbole —
When quiet and attentive we can trace
Our subtle and unspoken emotions —
But in our workaday ways our faces
Are serious and absorbed in our chores
Cogitating on mundane commotion
As we focus on faraway places
And much too often we find ourselves bored.

Hollywood actors
simulate sincerity
with lip-trembling clues
with watery eyes
with verisimilitude.

A crocodile doesn't show emotion
A snake can slither but it doesn't smile
An ostrich can scamper for miles and miles
Inexpressive in its locomotion
There are countless beings in the ocean
And most don't bother to demonstrate bile
As they eat each other in mindless style
A dolphin can be joyous in motion
An octopus is capable of play
An elephant shows wisdom in its eyes
A dog can be a source of sympathy
My Kitcat is frolicsome every day
Some animals are smart — and they don't lie —
They do lovable reciprocity.

We humans are
dubiously gifted with
politicians who
can deceive and accuse
innocent people with ease.

A holy person is liable to
Befuddle a novice by presenting
An odd statement of a nagging puzzling
Nature which the novice is supposed to
Ponder wholeheartedly and to come to
Absorb lovingly each of the words taking
The surface meaning and meditating
Over a day with nothing else to do
And as the mind naturally leaps from
Thought to thought to thought the absurdity
Of the teacher's remark asserts itself —
The eccentricity of the words worms
Itself deeper with an uncertainty
Whether the meaning will resolve itself.

If you wear shoes
with rubber soles
the whole world will
be covered with
rubber.

I'm not certain that a single-pointed
Concentration is the object of the
Exercise and I do suspect that the
Guru would like his words to be sampled
Like the bouquet of a fine wine inhaled
And absorbed throughout the hours of a
Day without the distracting snares of the
Frenzied rush of business complicated
By pressing problems needing solutions
Maneuvering crazy-making pressures
Burdened with a need for accomplishment —
But the guru does create the suspicion
That all of his nonsensical measures
Are only producing befuddlement.

When a pickpocket
encounters a saint
his only concern
resides in the saint's
pockets.

I'm sorry — it is hard to focus right now
I will do my best but I'm distracted
My poetry is being impacted
I want to do two things at once somehow
And I can't do either well anyhow
My phone is busy and I'm affected
Which is a thing I haven't expected
It's a situation that I allow
As I'm sitting at my desk trying to
Write poetry while also texting with
Women on Match.com — so that I am
Looking at my phone expectantly to
Finagle my talents as a wordsmith
And my head resembles a traffic jam.

The pacing of texts
is different from woman
to woman and it's
tricky to fashion the best
angle of approach with each.

Kitcat and I have been housemates for a
While and we understand each other well
And I can say he primarily dwells
Upon satisfying his appetite with a
Customary schedule and at times in the
Day he climbs on top of a small step stool
In the kitchen endeavoring to tell
Me that he is anticipating a
Serving of delicious treats which I keep
In a bag on the kitchen counter and
Then he yowls to summon my attention
And I am indulgent — though I don't leap
To placate him — but I lollygag and
Saunter and bellow to create tension.

Usually three
times in a day we do
a lion taming
routine — but who is training
whom is problematical.

How can I put my face to its best use?
Do I practice gestures with a mirror?
Can I make my sincerity clearer?
Should cordial expression be profuse?
Would passionate exhibitions seduce?
Could humble self-abnegation endear?
How should my curiosity appear?
And does subtlety produce the most juice?
When I observe Hollywood performers do
Their renditions of situations
They don't overplay their faces because —
Of course — they're comely and they don't have to
Impose their feelings with declarations
When elegant subtlety earns applause.

Perhaps I'd be much
happier if I forget
what my face does
and if I attend to
whatever is happening.

The window in front of my desk looks east
And there are oak trees to the west across
The street and the oak leaves are being tossed
By a wind finally having been released
And the leaves are falling making a feast
Of dissipation and I feel a loss
And I'm thinking how I can put across
The sweetness of melancholy increased
By the pace of descending oak leaves in
The air and the many trees before my
Eyes are already bare and their branches
Are moving in the wind to underpin
A tactile sense of disappearance tied
To patient curiosity that lives.

Just a few wispy
clouds moving southward give the
sky a pace and
a direction at odds with the
blustery movement of trees.

Oh! What my round bootlaces did to me
I'd walk around and they would come untied
Which was a constant slighting of my pride
With a forced feeding of humility
An unwanted idiosyncrasy
When all I wanted to do was to stride
And there I was frustrated standing astride
Sloppy laces — oh what idiocy —
And I'd have to bend over again in
Public places and retie the laces
Which seemed such an act of futility
And I couldn't be walking about in
Winter blizzards taking angry paces
With my laces trailing me shamefully.

A friend advised that
I had only to take the
rabbit ears of my
usual knot and double
knot and since then I do.

Don't think about what happened yesterday
And don't worry much about tomorrow
Wouldn't you rather belittle sorrow
To free your energy and get away
There's no use in fabricating doomsday
Settle yourself — and become a flambeau
If you're despondent then learn the banjo
Even responsible adults can play
You can surf the waves of your emotions
And while resting you may linger and watch
Disturbance dissipating before you
As it's all vibrating ceaseless motion
And nothing has to matter very much —
You need not be a miserable stew.

If only I could
learn how to relax just
when I wanted or
needed to then I could be
a harmless peaceful hippie.

It's not the same piece of winter sky that
I'm seeing outside the window as I'm
Breathing oxygen produced just on time
For this moment now and it isn't that
I'm insensitive or asleep or that
I'm unappreciative that winter rhymes
Year after year and that the seasons chime
Day after day but it's elusive that
I'm looking at the same twisty bare trees
And the so familiar high overcast
Sky and it seems that I've been here before —
Weary — still not knowing how to appease
A dreary restlessness — and yet a vast
Impending liberation is in store.

Looking past the same
bare branches — I remember —
it's a different sky
today and liberation
could happen in a blink.

Isn't it hilarious that so much
Energy goes into persuading a
Person to love you and I think it's a
Possibility that there's overmuch
Love available but that it is such
An elusive thing depending on a
Spontaneous connection that is a
Gift and all I can do is be in touch
With what I think is happening — even
Though it's true that I don't know — and isn't
It curious to play the role of a
Lost and lonely soul who does believe in
Surprises and to be one who doesn't
Quit and who is ready to be gaga.

Wanting love can be
a kind of hunger and so
I try to be as
light as a feather waiting
patiently to give my gift.

The thing I have to wrap my head around
Is the thought *nobody cares* which is a
Slap to a person's confidence and a
Blow to the ego which becomes a wound
When life's troubles appear as a beat down
And it seems that I am up against a
Tide of difficulty and I need a
Power greater than myself to face down
An impending sense of isolation
Of meaningless emptiness that can so
Easily take over a person's thought —
I am grateful for my incarnation
And am strong enough to take many blows
As I practice watching my train of thought.

Then I suppose that
the emptiness from which
everybody comes
is an indestructible
and curious *no-body*.

There is satisfaction in doing things
That are practical and tangible that
Everyone can grasp ahold of and that
They can appreciate which also springs
From accumulated talents and brings
A level of commercial reward that
Pays for all the necessary things that
Fill a household and takes away the sting
Of having to work so hard and I am
Thinking of a mason who works with bricks
And stone who applies his patience and his
Strength — a worthy workman using his hands
As I am sure he has mastered many tricks
Of his trade of which he's truly a whiz.

For three hours I
assembled an essay but
accidentally
deleted it with one
stupid tap on a keyboard.

It's not solely caffeine in my coffee
That I use to my advantage — and I'm
Sure the caffeine helps — but I know the time
Of the day when I have felicity
And I am most awake and it's easy
Then to connect my thoughts with words that rhyme
And then my emotions and grammar chime
Just when I'm having the most clarity
Because for most of the day I do my
Business on my own without the chance to
Use my words while I believe that life is
Best with conversation and I scrape by
Alone — as well as I might — but I do
Want to see what communication does.

I leverage
rhythmic energy
to communicate
with you who are
an open white page.

It's easy to blame politicians for
The screwed-up state of our society
As they take on responsibility
By simulating a show of candor
Knowing as they do it's hard to keep score
Of distant laggardly bureaucracy
Which creates societal entropy
While we citizens expect so much more
From our public servants and we tend to
Choose the politicians who are smooth at
Telling lies while we neglect to admit
That we would like to profit from a slew
Of subsidized government programs that
Can't last forever — as there are limits.

Those who exercise
power profit from
power — everyone
else squabbles over
scraps.

Do you suppose that he was serious
When he wrote those dozens of besotted
Sonnets in iambic bebop trotted
About as if he were delirious
With love which would be deleterious
To balance to be so tightly knotted
In confusion and to be so clotted
With passion appearing imperious
In one poem and then melancholic
In the next and isn't it curious
That he doesn't portray his lover with
Defined clarity which is symbolic
Of a fantasy and injurious
To the health of such an addled wordsmith.

Shakespeare's sonnets
are like the skull of Yorick
that Hamlet dug up
from the dirt — who can gauge
the jester's sincerity?

You know these sonnets are a fabrication
They're written in the spirit of a game
They're phantasmagoria without shame
As I am giving vent to my fixations
Where I can practice painless flirtations
Whereas real emotions can be a drain
And I would much rather play with the flame
Of a curious elucidation
And you may see each poem as a wall
Of words fitted tightly together like
The stones of Machu Picchu without
Mortar — or perhaps like the overall
Effect of a prosaic concrete dike
That says to a sea of boredom — keep out!

On every page of
this book there is a wall of
words wherein each word
does righteous duty without
any superfluity.

What does the whiteness of a page mean to
You as you turn the pages with the tips of
Your fingers as white is a color of
Purity and of being unsoiled to
The touch of the eye being easy to
Overlook as the words get the best of
Your attention and as the focus of
Curiosity the words proclaim to
You what is worthy of notice — but don't
Discount the quiet presence of paper
Sliced and so precisely weighted for the
Fingertips of readers because you don't
Recognize truth without the paper
Which is invisible — like the word "the".

Feathery clouds and
a new-fallen snow have a
soothing quality
so easy to overlook
against the pepper of life.

You have a story to tell and maybe
Your happiness comes in conversation
In simple and unhindered discussion
As the weight of experience is freed
And communication dispenses seeds
Of peace as you may escape delusions
Of all your self-punishing conclusions
As another person could set you free
With a healing of intimacy that
Dispenses with the need for caution as
There are people who can't be trusted but
Some of us are compatible with what
Feels so much like a hole in you and is
The burning of emptiness in the gut.

In my youth I met
a derelict old drunk who
asked me to write his
life's story but I didn't
have the energy for it.

For most people the holiday season —
Including Thanksgiving — is a time for
The gathering of family and for
The sharing of experience upon
The hardships that we don't have to dwell on
The getting over of life-numbing chores
And we have the chance to open the doors
Of our hearts to each other again on
Christmas and New Year's Day but for some of
Us there's a paradox of convention
That societal expectation makes
The spontaneous act of showing love
A difficult role that's full of tension
Inspiring a taste of sour grapes.

I'm grateful for the
Grinch who steals Christmas
for the elucidation
of the stubbornness
of the suffering.

There are deserts to cross on the way to
Liberation with the aspiration
With the impatience of expectation
That with mighty efforts I can accrue
The wisdom beyond wisdom and I do
The prescribed remedies for deflation
And I don't shirk my share of frustrations
And I have the resolve to see it through
Encountering the aftermath of the
Dissolution of my family that
Left me with a household full of items
Belonging to an ex-wife a son a
Daughter of trivial little things that
Bite me — what am I going to do with them?

I'm not ready for
the inspiration
of the memories
involved with every
trivial item.

An elephant is a ponderous brute
With provocative and curious eyes
It may be an impish elf in disguise
And it possesses a dexterous snoot
Which is a delicately touching snout
It makes use of its trunk to tantalize
To touch and caress and to socialize
And having such a limb must be a hoot
The elephant lumbers upon the earth
Its legs are like tree trunks with big round feet
Every footfall thuds and reverberates
Each echoing impact comes from its girth
It parades about in tuneful rhythm
Pounding about in a procession of beats
With thumping plopping steps that resonate.

The elephant can
hear the whopping of distant
elephants with the
sensitivity of its
attentive listening feet.

What would I do with an elephant's snout?
Could I turn the pages and read a book?
Or slice an onion with a knife and cook?
And turn a doorknob to get in and out?
And use a steering wheel to drive about?
Could I enclose a tulip's stem and pluck
Would I sniff a Coca-Cola and suck?
I'd swing it about if I were a lout
And could my elephant's appurtenance
Be an instrument of intimacy
Delicate enough to undo buttons
To unfasten bras with a nonchalance
To fondle soft breasts with intricacy
To probe inside of a bellybutton?

I guess the question
would revolve about whether
an elephant's trunk
would appear an enchanting
appendage on Match.com.

Every being possesses dignity
And I'm thinking of the worthy giraffe
Now you may be tempted to scoff and laugh
And read these lines for cheap hilarity
Which only shows your own barbarity
I am writing on the giraffe's behalf
And it deserves a witty epigraph
As it is an intriguing panoply
Giraffes don't care about your opinion
Giraffes embody elongated grace
Giraffes demonstrate curious caution
Giraffes exert a peaceful dominion
A giraffe has a respectable face
A giraffe is levity in motion.

To watch a giraffe
gallop over distance is
to see a loping
and a swinging grace that makes
locomotion beautiful.

It is not the most remarkable thing
About a giraffe and it looks puny
And it does appear a little loony
And if it chooses the giraffe could fling
It left and then if so inclined could zing
It right and when the giraffe is gloomy
It droops and when the giraffe is sunny
It swings and we could even say it sings
With happiness but it has prosaic
Use as the giraffe is assailed by flies
That tickle and bite the poor giraffe's rump
And there it is available to flick
The pesky flies before they even try
To bite — so the giraffe is not a grump.

The giraffe's plumy
tail appears exceedingly
laughable until
one sees it flick flies over
most of the giraffe's body.

He showers when he gets home at night so
He's free in the morning to wake and get
Out the door and he doesn't shave and lets
A week's worth of stubble grow and he goes
To work composed and I really don't know
How he can move without coffee and yet
That is what he does and he doesn't fret
Very much in his work-a-day tempo
Because he's done all the aspects of the
Job being a surveyor measuring
Distances and establishing order
About himself plotting points upon a
Grid and there's an ease in calculating
Numbers with no messes to get over.

If only people
in his life were as easy
to finagle as
numbers he wouldn't have to
grow loving roots into God.

I am attached to my morning shower
There are chores that I do before it
When waking I am only a halfwit
The minutes go by and I gain power
My brain gets going and my thoughts flower
Kitcat's hungry so I give him tidbits
I watch him run about — he doesn't quit —
When I don't feed him he does get sour
I traipse about the house for half an hour
Replenishing Kitcat's water and food
Taking care of his basement litter box
I read yesterday's poems and scour
Them for mistakes — I like my solitude —
My home resembles a childhood sandbox.

By the time I
enter the shower and
savor warm water
enveloping me my thoughts
are popping like popcorn.

Do you suffer from an attachment to
Your face being ever mindful of your
Appearance thinking it is a fixture
Of who you are that sticks to you like glue?
You can't escape no matter what you do —
And you do your best to create allure
To be genuine — but you are unsure —
Is your face only something you look through?
Is it even possible to think of
Who you are besides what you look like and
Can you imagine how differently
You would live without the idea of
Your appearance as if it were a brand
Which compromises elasticity?

How many hours
could you get by without a
mirror to make the
readjustments that you know
are absolutely needed?

We gather in libraries to read our
Poetry to each other handing out
Our poems and then we dangle our snouts
Over the pages to fuss and scour
Our verses trying not to be sour
Aiming to be helpful and not to spout
Piffle but to summon our best to sprout
Our creativity and to flower
In whichever way we choose to express
Because we want to use our freedom to
Say anything that we are moved to say
But how can we do that without finesse?
And I tend to be blind to my miscues
And it takes scrutiny to make headway.

Writing poetry
is like launching into an
acrobatic leap
and a writers' group performs
the job of a safety net.

I know I'm asking for trouble when I
Start reading profiles again but either
I act doing my best to be eager
Or I admit that I am too damn shy
And it's true that I'm not a quitting guy
So the goal becomes to be a seeker
While being mindful of my demeanor
But often all I can do is to sigh
While looking at girls on a dating app
Because no matter what I do it's so
That most of them don't bother to reply —
Yes — I know that is better than a slap
But I have to practice not feeling low —
It seems that the rules of hunting apply.

The object is not
to collect a harem but
to find one woman
who matches me well enough
to be a cozy couple.

There is quizzical Debbie to ponder
And she is not the one who is confused
But what she is doing has me bemused
She is a beauty which I can't ignore
With a sense of humor that I adore
My interest in her is already fused
But she leaves me feeling a little bruised
I can't determine what she has in store
She replies intermittently leaving
Me to dangle in between messages
Encouraging me by giving me her
Phone number but it is confusing
When I rouse myself and call she teases
By not answering — what should I infer?

She's agreed to meet
at India Palace after
the holidays which
is almost a month away
and does keep me lingering.

Sundays are my sanctuary when I
Can leave my bed at my leisure
And devote myself to mindful pleasure
Not having a work schedule to go by
When the heft of my business applies
I get to explore internal treasure
To plumb awareness and take my measure
And I am happy with what I come by
As I plant my bottom in my chair and
Fish for ideas in the air with the
View of my window — and every
Day mind is the game that I take in hand
And I know most of you would say — huh? —
Writing poetry is my reverie.

I am blessed by the
discovery that I can
lighten my mood by
playing with words and it's
fine being solitary.

I can imagine what it would be like
Having a girlfriend and devoting time
Nurturing each other trying to chime
Our emotions — and would I have to strike
A precarious balance not to spike
My poetry jazzing time? When I rhyme?
Could I be a boyfriend only part-time?
And I do hope that we could think alike
And give each other some necessary
Freedom because I can't imagine how
I could write with someone tapping or stomping
A foot behind me quite impatiently
With a furrowed forehead and angry brows
Devouring glowering souring.

Because once I sit
my rump in my chair time goes
by and I lose track
until it's late afternoon
and I've blown my energy.

The presence of the winter cold again
Can be a pleasurable sensation
A dash of bracing invigoration
It is a dance up to the edge of pain
And to partake of the season is sane
Winter can bring a touch of elation
One might even say it's a flirtation
With danger and I'm not one to complain
Except that I'd rather not meet winter
In my living room when my furnace stops
Working and I shiver trying to sleep
In a frosty bed and my breath appears
As ghostly vapor and I have to drop
Everything to fix it — I can't be cheap.

A fan went out in
my furnace and it cost me
$500
to fix it but winter was
banished from my living room.

I pine for female companionship but
Through painful experience I know by
Now that it does me no good to deny
The subtle hesitations of my gut
And to allow myself easy shortcuts —
Women say what they want and I comply
I am straightforward and I do not lie
And I guess it takes patience to abut
Myself with just the right woman who would
Appreciate me for who I am and whom
I could understand well enough without
Our having to argue and so we could
Grace each other and so we could assume
Love — without having to figure it out.

In America
I am wandering about
looking for a piece
of a scattered puzzle that
abuts on me perfectly.

How often do you look at things about
You before you stop noticing them as I
Am thinking of a sign that almost cries
"*Turn Off the Coffee Pot!*" which loses clout
Over time and so it does come about
That we do forget and afterward sigh
Because we don't remember — though we try —
We are not negligent — we are not louts —
The sign is something we don't think about
So the coffee burns into a hard crust
And has to be soaked chipped and then scoured —
Burnt coffee is difficult to get out —
The people at the church have lost their trust
It's true I think they have somewhat soured.

I think it's not a
bad idea to have on
hand a supply
of the glass pots easy to
dispose of from time to time.

The snow is falling in a steady pace
It is falling amid the homes and trees
Barren branches are swaying in a breeze
It is the morning but there's not a trace
Of the sun — the light is dim in this place
I am typing carefully on the keys
At the window watching snow at my ease
And I think the season is full of grace
Even as the color is erased from
The earth and there is no demarcation
Between the descending snow and the sky
And the scene will be dark for months to come
As this is the time for hibernation —
December is opposite from July.

This white paper page
represents new-fallen snow
and the ordered rows
of black letters on the page
stand for the barren branches.

The sun isn't visible so often
During winter and yet by mid-morning
The landscape is lighted — trees are moving
In the wind and the blusters aren't softened
By a touch of warmth and days are often
Devoid of obvious cheer and feeling
More than a little forbidding blending
Together over time and not softened
By the lively variety of growth
And yet the sun isn't really absent
And sometimes it appears as a shiny
Spot and — yes — the sky and sun are both
White — but the sun is certainly present
And it will be bright eventually.

Even behind clouds
the sun is incandescent
radiating heat
in every direction and
lighting a chilly day.

The mechanism of a furnace lies
Outside the sphere of my understanding
And mine is especially frustrating
Involving a magnitude of surprise
That it burns fuel oil and most of the guys
Who fix furnaces are discouraging
And my situation is perplexing
As the bulk of the profession applies
Itself only to gas furnaces but
With the use of my determination
I found a couple companies who work
With oil and though there wasn't a shortcut
I did experience a redemption
By utilizing an expert's artwork.

Charles is a wealth of
genial information
and he replaced a
fan and tuned my furnace and
now it hums musically.

The utterances of crows convey a
Conspicuous thrust of intelligence
Expressed insistently with emphasis
And it's tricky to know how much of a
Range of meaning is involved or of the
Sort of feelings — maybe not gentleness
And perhaps there isn't much eloquence —
And whatever they're expressing there's a
Guttural ruthlessness that seems to be
In play that implies that there's a pecking
Order within a tribal dynamic
And when I see them gather in a tree
I can't help but wonder what they're saying
And whether I could be sympathetic.

To hear a single
crow caw on a cold morning
and be answered by
another in the same tree
is to hear a weird language.

They fly and land and hop spryly around
The carcass on the road and in turn they
Stab and bite and swallow bits of squirrel
Meat and grudgingly they take wing to get

Out of the way of a passing car and
On another day five or six of them
Range about the yard assaulting the air
With their raspy voices as they fly from

The cottonwood to the apple tree to
The maple and it is apparent that
There is something going on in the
Company of the crows as they talk to

Each other alive to their own concerns
Being indifferent to outsiders.

People choose to call
a group of crows a murder
as there is the sense
of an occupation
about their eerie presence.

If they are the same size two crows appear
Identical as they share the same shape
And mannerisms and yet to them there
Are differences and to hear their pitch

Of guttural language is to feel like
An outsider hearing foreign banter
As there is intelligence conveying
Purposes and urgency and there is

Something going on and there are roles to
Be executed driven by other
Than human prerogatives and spurred by
Stimuli peculiar to the world of

Crows composed of a cooperative
Domination of a territory.

To be under the
gaze of a society
of crows is to feel
the touch of detached and
wary curiosity.

The movements of clouds over the spinning
Earth exerts a subtle influence on
My moods as I go about my business —
I do make it a practice to watch the

Clouds and the sunshine — when the sky is cast
Over with a white or a grayish pall
I fall under a spell and time drags and
Days merge and the gloom perpetuates a

Sense of dreary endurance to be borne
Which is merely the creation of my
Mind no more substantial than the water
Vapor composing the moving ceiling

Of cumbersome clouds showing me just how
Omnipotent vapor and thoughts can be.

The suspicion of
being trapped within a place
of confinement and
of being bound by the cold
of winter months is subtle.

But once the clouds dissipate and the sky
Is open to the sunlight again the
Weight of my oppression lifts and a thrill
Of joy arises and a clarity

Of detail engulfs me and I can see
The emerging lines of a jet's contrails
Slowly spreading over the sky to be
Crossed by another pair of contrails and

When I absorb the foot of new-fallen
Snow I can rejoice with the crisp shadows
Of crooked trees upon the pristine white
And there are the sparkling crystals that are

Refracting rainbow points of sunlight that
Make me imagine a blanket of jewels.

The press of events
within human involvement
overwhelms the touch
of what the sky is doing
until one notices it.

The ordeal of moving the snow off of
My Mom's driveway would be trivial were
It not for the fact that the big blower
Won't start and I've had to resort to a

Puny electric thing that looks like a
Toy and I don't know why the prodigy
Inventers couldn't fashion plugs that stay
Connected but they didn't so I swore

And had to bend over tiredly to
Insert the prongs into the plug again
Being careful not stumble upon
The tangled length of cord trailing behind

Me as the silly and impotent maw
Took forever to do its simple work.

The thing threw snow half
the width of the driveway
which made a heap of
snow double the snowfall which
was a joy to deal with.

How can the mixing of the sky and earth
Be captured with words on paper other
Than in play as yesterday it seemed that
A cloud had settled in the neighborhood

And swallowed the white fence the homes the bare
Trees as the snow on the ground melted and
A mist painted the branches and twigs gray
And today the pale grass appears again

And fine grains of snow are curling in the
Air and coming from a sky without height
As there is no demarcation between
The sky and the snow but there is a glow

About the sky and the crooked branches
Amid the snow are swaying in blusters.

It is a scene of
fire earth water and air
mixed together as
93 million miles off
the sun keeps on combusting.

It has occurred to me that I haven't
Adequately expressed gratitude to
You for the years of attention you gave
To my emailed poems — you read every

One — and you wrote encouraging notes in
Reply faithfully every morning and
I get up early but you rise before
Me and reading my poetry must have

Been one of the first things you did for years
And the magnitude of such a heartfelt
Gift strikes me now that you've ceased reading them
Because I did I suppose finally

Exhaust you — which doesn't reflect on you
But on me — as you are ever loving.

By the way
you missed the
hundreds of
rhymed sonnets
I've written.

I am a traveler on the earth though
I don't often leave the neighborhood and
There are times when fear and isolation
Occupy my thoughts and gloom weighs
heavy

On me and I know that I know that such
Oppressions will pass but that doesn't make
The sad hours easier and then the mood
Shifts and the extent of distance appears

And I can see again with clarity
To far horizons and the local
Crows lose their spectral quality and when
I see a crow taking funny steps on

The frozen ground with its scrawny legs I
See a fellow being making its way.

I am human
like any other — riding
waves — being
someone doing something
thinking I'm going somewhere.

In a quest to buy a new snow blower
I went to Bayport Printing House to talk
To a mechanical genius I know
Who just happened to buy one last week at

Lowes where there are Ariens or Craftsman brands
To choose from and I went to Lowes and saw
The differences between price and size
And I asked whether they deliver to

Homes — and then I checked the machines on sale
At Menards and discovered the laggards
There deliver but they're too lazy to
Assemble the blower so they drop off

The blower in a weighty box leaving
The customer with an unpleasant chore.

My nuts and bolts
genius said that a
maintained blower
can be expected to last
fifteen to twenty years.

Whether I can do my chores without fuss
Is a challenge for my best effort — and
The mowing of the grass about my house
In summer is pleasant exercise now —

Though for several years facing the doubtful
Prospect that the blower would start at Mom's
House has made every impending snowstorm
An occasion of possible doom — but

The weight of living in Minnesota
Where snowplows are constantly scraping the
Streets and thrusting heaps of snow aside — where
The burden of clearing snow with an old

Machine is lifting from my shoulders — helps
To turn an ordeal into easeful joy.

Doing things well is
easier with the right tools
and the prospect of
having a new snow blower
helps me to laugh with winter.

I put the broken-down blower by the
Curb as two different guys advised and
When I returned this morning the two-stroke
High-pitched roaring squat and wide red little

Monster that for twenty years spewed snow was
Gone as someone driving by is betting
He can fix it or use parts of it and I'm
Grateful I didn't have to transport it

Or pay to have it removed and I don't
Know much about mechanics but I
Got clever at working around the quirks that
Signaled its slow disintegration as

Everything weakens and then falls apart
And I hope to outlast the next blower.

The screws that held its
plastic cover in place were
set aside and lost
winters ago when I swapped
spark plugs one sub-zero day.

We should have gratitude for nobody
Nobody is genuinely honest
Nobody is passionately sincere
Nobody is reliably helpful

If you want love nobody can help you
Intimacy is found with nobody
When you are lonely nobody is here
Nobody completely understands you

Nobody holds the planets in orbit
Nobody causes the sun's combustion
Nobody created all kinds of birds
At heart nobody is mysterious

When you need answers to questions you can't
Articulate — please — turn to nobody.

Beyond every
wavy spinning quark
is nobody.

With two sisters inside the bathroom the
Preteen girl was happy lying inside
Of the bathtub and she smiled and held a
Stuffed bear and I read the headline about

Tornadoes in Kentucky and glimpsed the
Photo and I didn't pause to think but
Later I watched a TV news report
And realized mere moments after that

Photo was snapped the house was torn to bits
And that girl was wrenched by the wind and hurled
A great distance and found dead — and from the
Cheerful innocence expressed in her face

One might guess that she believed that the rush
To the bathroom was no more than a game.

The report revealed
that girl suffered from a
diseased liver and
yet she was a being of
angelic visitation.

I believe in the love inside of me
Though I have not been very skillful in
Its expression as my love is suppressed
By cruel whispers of unworthiness that

Burden my thoughts and as I hunger for
Affirmation in the behavior and
The expressions of others toward me I
Guess that the vibes I emanate are an

Obstruction — but my predicament is
Balanced by patience and pluck and by a
Practice of gentleness with others who
Don't know of my occasional anguish

Which amounts to a self-imposed sense of
Unique and befuddled separation.

I think the fire of
my attention is burning
away the burden
of the propensities of
the negations of my thoughts.

I think my love finds fruitful expression
In the dogged persistence with which I
Gather with people who were drunks and with
People who love people who are drunks and

I do no more with them than to share the
Experience of being an ex-drunk
Who could be a voracious drunk again
If I stop the practice of spiritual

Jujitsu — we celebrate together
Our mutual vulnerability
And somehow in the exchange of our words
We find the strength and hope to live apart

From addiction — and most of what I do
In our meetings is to simply listen.

One finds in our groups
an honest expression of
the attitudes and
emotions that are burdened
and our humor is magic.

I see the Imperial Chinese designs
On the plastic placemats underneath the
Rice cooker inside a cupboard in the
Kitchen which prompts a pang of emotion

About the delicious meals my then-wife
Made over years when our kids were growing
And attending public schools in Stillwater
While I was busy being a husband a

Dad a printer an editor and the
Sorrow of the loss of those days is mixed
With sweetness as I know we did our best
And that the plastic placemats are symbols

Of how we lived — each of us comes away
With different patterns of memory.

These worthless things
are of no further use
and yet the thought
of throwing them out
is so painful.

Imagine the imperative imposed
By the growth of a horn positioned in
The center of your long snout between your
Eyes which you couldn't directly see

But could only feel the imposition
Of its weight yet from looking at others
In your own herd who had the thing you would
Easily assume that you had it too

And relative to other animals
You'd know you were a brute with a barrel
Chest and muscled legs that pound and thunder
The earth when you trot and your eyesight is

Poor while your sense of smell is good but you
Wouldn't be aware of those distinctions.

If you were a
rhinoceros
how much of you
would be determined
by your horn?

If I were a brute flexing my brawny
Legs in a trot plopping my flat feet on
The earth I would take pride in my weighty
Barbarity knowing nobody could

Knock me over and I would swing my head
Poised to charge and apply my heavy horn
To interlopers and I don't suppose
Much diligence would be directed to

The flicking of my tail which serves only
To cover a puckering backside but
I think my nostrils would be paramount
As I'd have a mighty appetite to

Satisfy and I would follow my nose
Sniffing for delicious edible plants.

Rolling in the mud
would be luxurious and
useful for adding
a layer of protection
against the biting of flies.

If you were mostly a humanoid but
Were born with a rhinoceros horn just
Above your eyes and you were heavy with
Thick muscled legs and two rhinoceros

Flat feet could you live harmoniously
Among people — apart from how they would
Behave toward you — do you suppose you'd be
Disposed to sudden bursts of temper and

Could you escape the preoccupation
Of being so different and could you
Cope with mirrors and would you be able
To savor a passion for symphony

Orchestras and gourmet recipes or
Would you adopt criminal tendencies?

Just having the
rhinoceros feet would
be enough to skew
your life — could you safely
partake of ballroom dancing?

Love gets mixed up in everyday business
As I'm doing the pattern of my life
Needing to do things on a schedule that
Takes my energy as there's often a

Problem like being behind a slow car
When I want to drive quickly — while my
Thoughts do return to a person who
I care about who I'm not able to

Meet as often as I'd like and I have the
Compulsivity of desire — with the
Doubt her adoration for me equals
Mine for her — which amounts to a yearning

That isn't satisfied — and I'm not sure
That this "so-called" love is durable love.

There is a thirsting
for something or someone that
is proportional
to denial of access —
which makes desire powerful.

I can turn my confusion to the way
I choose to do the patterns of my day
Including the gibberish I lavish
On Kitcat who thereafter excitedly

Gallops through the house — and to the pleasure
Of pedaling my stationary bike
While listening to Alan Watts my beatnik
Guru expostulating the *dharma* —

And to the fascination found in the
Subtle manifestations of snow and
The puzzling mentality of crows — and
The birth of a new day as seen from the

View of the valley at Pioneer Park
When the sun spangles the clouds with brilliance.

Love spills quietly
unappreciated and
unconsciously from
me as I merge myself in
the world and feel a kinship.

After I struggled starting the machine
When I failed to understand that a key
Needed to be inserted I got the
New snow "thrower" going and feel the strong

Torque of it — even at a slow setting —
And the handle grips keep me further at
A distance than I'm used to and I have
To muscle it roughly around corners

As it's bursting with power and wavers
From side to side — which I will control with
Practice — and the metal skids of it bounce
Over the broken-down pebbly parts of

The driveway — and the first pirouette with
An inch of fluffy snow goes well enough.

The machine is built
For moving heaps of snow and
leaves behind it a
fine layer of snow that will
Need scraping with a shovel.

When earplugs lessen stimuli beyond
The workings of my body I can hear
The beating of my heart and listen to
Its rapid and constant sound and I can

Also follow the inhalation of
My breath as it enters my nostrils and
Swells my chest and then the exhalation
Releases and relaxes my body

And I am never separate from these
Life-empowering rhythms and when the
Frenzy of thought captures the attention
Of my mind it's a comfort to know that

I always have the simplicity of
Obtaining peace — in my breath and heartbeats.

I have to quiet
myself and separate my
attention from the
lure of compulsivity
to follow breath and heartbeats.

This is the morning of the solstice when
The dance between the earth and sun changes
And the northern hemisphere obtains an
Increasing portion of sunlight each day

And the cyclical movement of the earth
Isn't obvious as it's happening
But the ebbing and flowing of life is
Never separate from its pattern as

Life consists of rhythms within rhythms
And the urgency of getting things done
In the human world has its rightful place
But it's helpful to know I don't have

To earn either my beating heart and breath
Or the solstices — as they are all gifts.

Clouds rain snow fog dew
springs rills creeks streams rivers
rapids river falls
are life-affirming patterns
of the sky earth and oceans.

This is an animal of glory and
Style displaying a train of feathers and
A royal crest on its head and it has
Crystals in its feathers that shimmer in

Sunlight with a stunning ensemble of
Iridescence of yellow and brown and black
And teal and most prominently of blue
And green and it does flourish and flaunt

And flounce and unfold its train of feathers
Like a Japanese fan swiftly spreading
And revealing a hypnotic array
Of jewel eyes appearing suddenly like

Some unearthly Hindu deity that
Casts a spell and astonishes one's soul.

The male peacock shakes
his iridescent feathers
with jewel eyes and
emits a vibration that
jangles the female's crest.

What do you make of the unearthly gloss
Of the peacock as it's not prideful nor
Vain and takes its business of foraging
For subsistence and its rituals of

Procreation in stride and it doesn't
Dwell on its superfluity and is
Not aware of the hypnotic spell it
Casts on people prompting fascination

As it becomes a symbol of regal
Beauty bespeaking vainglorious pomp
As an excess of sensuality
While we make a fetish of the finding

Of a single peacock feather as if
Its possession portended good fortune?

No craftsman sculptor
designer jeweler
painter or poet
could have conceived of
a peacock's feather.

Lily the calico cat was left by
Herself last night and when I arrive at
My desk she grumbles her meows with an
Insistence that isn't normal and as

I'm sitting and typing she's daintily
Stepping on the scattered sheets of paper
And pens and round stones and books that are strewn
On the desk in front of the window and

The footing is precarious but she
Manages gracefully though she bumps and
Just about upends a thermos of
Coffee before I catch it as she rubs

Herself under my nose and chin brushing
Against my growing beard making it itch.

Mom is visiting
her grandkids overnight on
Christmas day and
Lily has abandoned her
usual indifference.

Whatever it was that went bang billions
Of years ago when the temperature
Reached 1,000 trillion degrees Celsius
Nobody was here to see it and it

Did happen silently as sound depends
On an atmosphere to be transmitted
And there was no space and there was no time
Because space and time depend on bits of

Something to be strewn about within the
Reach of emptiness before they arise
And so the human mind can't conceive of
The void inside the Big Bang except to

Say that it happened nowhere consisted
Of nothing and that nobody did it.

What happened
is continuing
everywhere
simultaneously
now.

Hollywood directors don't do justice
To the eerie realities of the
Alien worlds that exist within our
Solar system on Saturn's largest moon

Titan which has an almost endless sea
Of icy ethane and methane under
An atmosphere of an unbreathable
Nitrogen gas and whatever landmass

There would be consists of floating islands
Of ice and ground covered in an ethane
Snow and the color palette would range from
White with tinges of blue to bluish white

Which would make for beautiful sunrises
But nobody lingers to paint the scene.

Words on paper
may vaguely sketch aspects
of the appearance
of Titan but words belong
to humanity on Earth.

I'm using the tool of meditation
To throw off identification with
My ego as a separate something
But the impetus of the discipline

Somehow gets in the way as it's tricky
To relax and to let liberation
Happen of itself — I am playing with
Words to clarify my opinions and

Emotions and intentions while I know
That words are intellectual catnip
Which help to direct me but of themselves
Words won't open the gate to *satori*

Which brings to mind the vermillion *Tori*
Gates that the Japanese make for their shrines.

A *Tori* gate is
the simplest structure of
two upright posts
two crossing beams — making an
entrance into the sacred.

I have come to love the use of words as
Nothing is more pleasurable than to
Craft a line that is clear and concise and
That's easily understood and spoken

And I like to contain my poetry
Within ten syllable lines as if the
Form were rigid while the nuances of
Meaning were liquid which I pour into

Any arbitrary vessel of my
Choosing as if the sonnet were made of
Crystal and the essence of the words were
Pure water free of the impurities

Of redundancy and opacity
With an illusion of the taste of no taste.

Of course a poet
can't keep a fiddling ego
out of the poem
which is why I strum tunes of
self-deprecating humor.

For those with eyes to see the landscape in
Winter is dominated by the wild
Gesticulation of the leafless trees
Conveyed over distance in the drab shades

Of grayish brown and if you would like to
Sample an undomesticated and
Undiluted portrayal of what cosmic
Energy looks like attend to the shapes

Of branches and twigs turning and twisting
In a concatenation of angles
Of bizarre directions as if the growth
Of trees were spontaneous explosions

Devoid of any sense of symmetry —
Except each tree is balanced by its roots.

Yet there are
oaks maple apple
magnolia and pine
and each kind is
distinctive.

Matsuo Basho was a Japanese poet
Who could capture the whole cosmos in a
Bowl the Japanese use for drinking tea
Because he could listen and watch without

Any obstruction of thought getting in
The way so when he saw an old pond and
A frog and he watched the frog jump in the
Pond the plop of the sound of the water

Reverberates as clearly today through
The centuries — when he heard the blusters
Of the rain spattering the banana
Leaf beside his hut we too can hear the

Beginning of the rain as it blows in the
Wind and drops upon the resonate leaf.

The sounds of a frog
and water and wind
and rain and of a
banana leaf need
no translation.

Whatever did go bang billions of years
Ago began motion and the pages
That you are turning came from a tree that
Gained life from minerals in the soil and

From sunshine in the air — which cannot be
Separated from the thing that went bang —
The words on the pages communicate
Thoughts and thoughts do share the same source as the

Parrots in South American jungles —
Oceans and mountains — ethane and methane
Seas on Titan — unknown phenomena
On some 1,000 trillion galaxies —

Underlying phenomena is the
Unborn and undying liberation.

Thoughts arise
from quiet interludes
of simplest observation
pregnant with life.

With both of the dates that I've finagled
Inside of a month each needed to be
Rescheduled a day before and one was
Rejiggered several times — and I am

Elated to adjust and to swallow
Disappointment with grace as behaving
Otherwise is futile — though I wish things
Were easier — the first woman is a

Writer and ex-drunk like me so we share
A common lingo but sadly there was
No spark — but the other has a saucy
Ukrainian accent and she is a

Beauty and she is a meditator —
But she is also somewhat tentative.

I don't know whether
her standoffishness
is native to her
personality or is
a boundary to be crossed.

I've gotten over my self-consciousness
On first dates and I can present myself
Easefully spontaneously with words
And depending on her I am able

To be funny or to leverage my
Unusual enthusiasms my
Foreign travels my curiosity
But the introduction is a balancing

Act and I'm meeting a unique person
As she is a different droplet of
The same cosmos offering a new
Reflection of what there is and I would

Like to know whether we are similar
Harmonious and complimentary.

I have no clue what's
going to happen
and I look forward
to meeting the right
woman.

What is the pith inside of loneliness?
Does it come only from an absence of
Female companionship? Is it about
A disconnection from the status games

And the political slant that people
Impose? Can I lay the blame off on my
Parents for the things they did and didn't
Do? Does alcoholism have any

Weight after I've been sober for decades?
I need a particular type of touch
And hunger for facial expressions
I want the caress of another's eyes

It is good to exchange lighthearted words
And it would be great to share in a joke.

I am a human
who wrestles with
the separation
sickness of the ego and
hungers for liberation.

Think of the succeeding pages layered
One over another as the days of
Winter and the white of paper is like
A succession of snowy days wherein

The snow isn't soiled and the scenery
Is pristine and the weight of the cold burns
The skin and yet allows for the comfort
Of wearing warm clothes balanced by quiet

In which the sound of cars resonates in
The air differently from summer noise
Which is a numbing concatenation —
And doesn't the winter cast a spell and

Isn't it odd to gaze at the frozen
Yet wild gesticulation of bare trees?

Crows and cardinals
squirrels grasping ahold of
the creases of the
bark of the barren trees bring
a prominence to the trees.

A desk a window and snow on the hedge
Just a couple of feet outside are a
Point of departure and the glowing clouds
Swallow distance and yet there is freedom

To balance my sense of myself wherein
Time flows behind me like the frothy wake
Of a ship and if I choose what happened
Yesterday can be a weight on my mind

And if I'm energized and nimble this
Moment imposes itself quietly
And eyes that see are the apertures through
Which the cosmos is gazing at itself

And I know that even when I'm angry
Or afraid it is fitting to be here now.

Quiet emptiness
undergirds hubbub
concatenation
and I hold in my being
a return ticket to now.

I do like saying hippopotamus
Because it is a buoyant happy sound
The first two syllables kind of tiptoe
The last three stampede pell-mell together

Hip-po-potamus

Just saying the word lightens my spirit
And for fun I pop every single p

Hi**pp**o**p**otamus

I say it with a rising inflection

Hippo*potamus*

And then with a sinking inflection

*Hippo*potamus

It goes with a maniacal creature
A dopey jowly roly-poly brute
A rather irascible animal
With a small tail and ears — and a huge mouth

When I have my next opportunity
I do intend to say it happily.

The problem is in
casual conversation
I don't remember
ever having had the chance
to say hi**p**-**p**o-***p**otamus*.

Monkey Mind

You must not think about monkeys this week
Said the guru to his disciple and
The disciple thought "how easy as I
So seldom think about monkeys" but while

Walking home baboons came to mind and when
Meditating chimpanzees bothered him
And gorillas disturbed his dreams and at
Breakfast mountain monkeys with red bottoms

Troubled him and so it went for a week
And the disciple became angry and
Said to the guru "You told me not to
Think about monkeys knowing that saying

So would make me obsessed with monkeys" and
The guru smiled and said "Now you understand."

I have resolved as
a Minnesotan who does
remove the snow from
driveways that I simply won't
think about snow this winter.

I shoveled the light snow from the driveways in
In the dark of New Year's Eve because the
Forecasted temps were for brutal cold which
I wanted to avoid — I finished off the

Year watching a video and went to
Bed an hour before midnight — inside
My dreams there were lynxes and cheetahs and
Cougars and each of the cats ran in its

Own style — before waking I saw robots
Dancing in the air — I awoke refreshed
To hear Kitcat galloping through the house
Which he does apart from predatory

Impulse but with sudden bursts of nonsense
And an abundance of enthusiasm.

The morning sky of
New Year's Day is clear of
clouds — all sorts of
birds are darting between the
trees — fresh snow is very bright.

I am bored and browse the Internet seeing
A site of Old West photos that displays
The Dalton Gang shot dead and laid on boards
After they had failed to rob the bank in

1892 Coffeyville Kansas
And there are Buffalo Bill and Wild Bill
Hickok and then I observe a youthful
Face without whiskers and I notice her

Beautiful hair and womanly form clothed
In cowboy gear with hat and boots and
She holds a Henry repeating rifle —
Her face and relaxed shoulders express a

Confidence at home on the frontier and
Oh! how easily I could have loved her.

She robbed stagecoaches
was captured and imprisoned
for several years
in the 1890s the
caption barely explains.

A photograph from 1863
Shows samurai Koboto Santaro
Wearing a blue vest and plated armor —
The caption says that this type of armor

Appeared in fourth century Korea
Or China — it looks sophisticated
And lightweight — the helmet is festooned with
Gold wings and a disk which could be either

The sun or moon — his face is protected
By a hardened mask exaggerated
With the brutal features of a demon
And only a small portion of skin is

Visible about his eyes — he handles
A large white ceremonial tassel.

The two katana slung
within easy grasp of
the samurai bespeak
a keen lethality.

A recording of my beatnik guru
Alan Watts leads me to think that I've grasped
The point while I am pedaling hard on
My stationary bike in my living

Room as he simply says that it is a
Metaphysical truth that every thing
Has an inside and an outside and yet
The boundary between them isn't real

And happenings can't be separated
Into isolated events and when
One sees into the truth of the nature
Of things then the squirming of the frightened

Ego is unnecessary because
It's no more substantial than a bubble.

The problem is I
can't stop feeling that I'm
somebody going
somewhere progressing even
on a stationary bike.

The predicament comes at 3 a.m.
When I awake and can't return to sleep
And if I could return to sleep that would
Be a skillful trick of liberation —

I am tense from thinking about what
Happened yesterday and also about
What could happen tomorrow — I know such
Thinking is futile and yet my body

Turns and my mind is busy — trying to
Relax isn't relaxing — the more I
Try the more enmeshed I am — energy
Simmers but my thoughts lack the potency

Of spontaneous choice and as I yearn
For sleep I watch my mind work uselessly.

I cannot do what
I'd like to do but can't stop
trying to do it
as I don't yet know how to
make effortless effort.

I drove to a clinic in White Bear Lake
To get the booster shot of the vaccine
For COVID-19 as the numbers of
Cases of the latest variant of

The virus are exploding not only
In America but around the world
While it's a good sign that this version is
Much more infectious but also much less

Deadly signaling perhaps that every
Person will get it eventually
But it will be no more dangerous than
A cold so that we can throw away our

Masks and the bureaucrats can stop forcing
People to take vaccines that aren't working.

Closing businesses
demanding the wearing of
ineffective masks
were measures driven by fear
as the virus virused.

Alan Watts describes the trick of letting
Go of an arrow without conscious thought
As the best archers do aim and release
Spontaneously without a tangle

Of thought — if one aims and afterward
Decides to let go a complication
Arises — one has to decide when to
Decide — which becomes a predicament —

I aim for liberation but might be
Happy with relaxation — I seek love
But may be satisfied with companions —
I loiter over a keyboard at a

Window waiting for ethereal words
But I'll type this ordinary poem.

The shadows of trees
have lengthened on the snow on
the ground and on the
roofs of homes until the sun
sinks and all the shadows merge.

Sun sinks
Shadows of trees on snow merge —
crow is on a branch.

—*Tekkan*

www.ingramcontent.com/pod-product-compliance
Lightning Source LLC
Chambersburg PA
CBHW040419100526
44589CB00021B/2755